Fertility, female employment
and policy measures in Hungary

Women, Work and Development, 6

Fertility, female employment and policy measures in Hungary

Barnabás Barta, András Klinger,
Károly Miltényi and György Vukovich

Published with the financial support of the
United Nations Fund for Population Activities
(UNFPA)

International Labour Organisation   Geneva

ISBN 92-2-103624-3
ISSN 0253-2042

First published 1984

Printed by the International Labour Office, Geneva, Switzerland

Preface

It is well known that in Eastern European socialist countries fertility rates fell rapidly after the post-war baby boom and at the same time, increasing numbers of women became economically active. Not as well known is that the overall decline of fertility rates in many Eastern European countries (including Hungary) has been interspersed with periods of significant increases and decreases.

Warned by declining birth rates and at the same time desiring that women be able to join and/or remain in the active labour force, these governments have introduced major new policy measures aimed at encouraging fertility and facilitating the combination of motherhood with work outside the home. Has women's employment been an important factor affecting fertility? Are there other factors contributing to lower fertility?

The present monograph addresses these and other questions in a detailed study of the case of Hungary. Factors related to fertility include, in particular, women's employment and pronatalist, demographic and labour market policy measures of the government. This monograph presents not only demographic and employment data for the Hungarian population as a whole, but also gives interesting results of KAP (Knowledge, Attitude and Practice of Family Planning) surveys, panel surveys of marriage cohorts, and time budget studies.

Table of Contents

INTRODUCTION[1]

The present monograph reviews current work on factors influencing fertility and female economic activity in Hungary.

Chapter 1 outlines fertility trends over the last 36 years. Despite fluctuations in the crude birth rate, the general fertility rate and the total fertility rate, there has been an overall decrease in fertility over this period which is likely to last until the end of the 1980s. In addition, the net reproduction rate, which has been under one for the greater part of the last 36 years, indicates that a population decrease can be expected in the long run.

In Chapter 2, the main elements of social and population policy are reviewed as a background to the discussions in the following chapters on the relationship between fertility and fertility determinants including female economic activity. The impact of the child-care allowance on socio-economic life is noted in particular.

Chapter 3 examines the increase in female economic activity during the period and the influence of this increased economic activity on fertility levels, finding that most of the decline in fertility is associated with the increasing proportion of working women amongst women of reproductive age. However, certain fluctuations in the fertility of working women suggest that having children (usually no more than two) may not be an obstacle to female economic activity. The effects on fertility levels of changes in female educational levels and of changes in industrial and occupational structure are also discussed.

The trends noted in Chapter 3 have led to several studies on fertility attitudes and practices, and the main results of these studies are given in Chapter 4. These include a retrospective study started in 1958, two longitudinal marriage studies started in 1966 and 1974, and two time budget studies. The extent to which family planning is used is examined, together with various items which have an influence on desired family size. The practice of birth control in its various forms is then reviewed. And finally, the effect of the stability of marriage on family size and the possible negative influence of time spent by women on household duties are discussed.

Chapter 5 examines attitudes and opinions related to fertility determinants, based mainly on results of a survey carried out in 1978 by the Demographic Research Institute of the Hungarian Central Statistical Office. These attitudes are broadly grouped as follows: first, the advantages and disadvantages of having children and whether or not they affect economic activity; second, the effect of child-care allowance on family life and some suggestions as to how its scope could be broadened; third, the role institutions play in assisting mothers with children; fourth, the extent to which housing conditions influence the family; and finally the mother's unequal share of household work and some indications as to how a more equal division of labour could be brought about.

Notes

1 We would like to acknowledge the assistance of Lajos Bárány, Péter Józan, Ferenc Kamarás, József Kepecs, Judit Nagy and Marietta Pongrácz, all of the Hungarian Statistical Office.

We would also like to express our appreciation for the comments and support of Catherine Hein, Richard Anker and the ILO.

Chapter 1

FERTILITY TRENDS

In Hungary, as in central, eastern and southern Europe, the demographic transition occurred more than 50 years later than in some western and northern countries of Europe. In Hungary this transition, and the subsequent decrease in fertility, began in the middle of the last century. Although the general fall in the crude live birth rate was observed only from the 1880s onwards, the gradual decline of the birth rate in Budapest and in some regions began 30-50 years earlier. References in the then-contemporary literature indicate that the practice of birth control within marriage began to spread in the middle of the last century.

Although the development of fertility trends in the hundred-year period after 1880 will be touched on in this chapter, the 36-year period since the end of the Second World War will be treated in detail.

1. Births

In 1880, the crude live birth rate[1] was over 44 per thousand population and by the turn of the century it had decreased to just under 40 per thousand (see table 1.5). This declining trend continued with slight fluctuations in the following decades, and was also generally characteristic of the period after the Second World War. The birth rates of the last 36 years, however, show great fluctuations. In the second half of the 1940s, the birth rate was higher than in the previous 10 years and stabilised at around 20-21 per thousand. Due to very strict administrative measures limiting abortion, the first baby boom occurred in 1953-55, and reached its peak in 1954 when the crude live birth rate rose to 23 per thousand. After this, partly due to the after-effect of births in 1953-55 and partly under the impact of the legalisation of induced abortions, the number and rate of births began to decrease. The minimum was attained in 1962 with a crude birth rate of 12.9 per thousand; in 1962 the absolute number of live-born children was lower by over 93,000 (i.e. by 48 per cent) than in 1954. A very low level (13.1 per thousand) was also characteristic of the following three years.

After 1966, birth rates increased to a certain extent, but this increase was followed by another stagnation with fertility rates below replacement level until 1973 (when the net reproduction rate was below one). To increase willingness to give birth to children, extensive new population policy measures were adopted in 1973. These are described in detail in Chapter 2. The favourable impact of these measures was soon felt. A new baby boom occurred, partly as a result of these population policy measures and partly due to the fact that the large female cohorts born at the time of the baby boom of 1953-55 gave birth to their first and/or second children. This baby boom began in 1974 and reached its maximum (a crude live birth rate of 18.4 per thousand) the following year. However, a renewed decline took place after that and in 1980 the number and crude rate (13.6 per thousand) of live births was approximately 25 per cent lower than in 1975. According to recent projections, the decrease in fertility will last until the end of the 1980s. One of the reasons is that in this period the marriage rates and the birth rates will be determined by the small female cohorts born in the first half of the 1960s. This means that approximately until the end of the 1980s the crude birth rate will be even lower than the very low value observed in the first half of the 1960s.

2. Fertility Rates

The trends in the general fertility rate (i.e. the ratio of live births to the number of 15-49 year old females) and the total fertility rate (i.e. an estimate of the number of live births women will have during their lifetime) were practically the same as those of the crude birth rate but their fluctuation was smaller. This is largely due to the fact that the fluctuation of birth rates is affected not only by fertility but also by changes in the number and composition of the female population of reproductive age.

The rapid decline in fertility rates between the mid-1950s and the mid-1960s is fairly typical of European socialist countries. In Western Europe and North America, on the other hand, fertility rates fell sharply mainly as from the mid-1960s. By 1980, the total fertility rate of the United States was 1.9, the same as in Hungary. It can be noted that compared to other European socialist countries, fertility rates in Hungary have tended to be low throughout this century and in 1980 only East Germany had a lower rate.

Great changes can be observed in the distribution of live births by age of mother. The most important feature is the continuous decrease in the average generation length due mainly to the large decrease in the fertility of older women. At the beginning of the century, approximately 24 per cent of fertility each year was to women 20-24 years old; in the 1930s this proportion was around 28 per cent after which it rose to about 41 per cent. Thus, for the last 50 years the highest birth rate has been observed among females aged 20-24 years. At the same time the proportion of fertility attributable to women 35 years old and above fell from about 19 per cent to about 4 per cent (see table 1.1).

Changes in overall fertility levels in Hungary are affected primarily by the fertility rate of married females aged 20-24 years. After the baby boom of the early 1950s, their fertility rate decreased fairly steadily until the beginning of the 1960s. From 1963, their fertility rate slightly increased but after 1974-76, when fertility was also relatively high in the other age groups, their fertility rate decreased from year to year and the 1980 value (158.6 per thousand) was 14 per cent lower than in 1975.

Summarising results on fertility by age of women, it can be said that in Hungary, as in other European socialist countries, the fertility of younger married women plays a decisive role in determining the total number of births. In addition, the fertility of

- 4 -

Table 1.1: Age-specific live birth rates by age of mother

Year	15-19	20-24	25-29	30-34	35-39	40-44	45-49	General fertility rate	Total fertility rate
1901*	64	257	277	191		42		154	5.32
1910-11*	64	248	248	170		36		144	4.86
1921	40.7	202.0	212.1	126.7		25.2		116.8	3.80
1930-31	40.9	158.5	151.8	110.7	74.8	27.5	2.9	88.0	2.84
1940-41	41.1	144.9	134.5	95.8	56.6	20.5	2.0	71.3	2.48
1948-49	46.5	163.0	137.7	88.5	54.0	19.8	1.7	75.7	2.56
1952	48.1	165.3	135.4	85.3	43.5	16.2	1.2	73.5	2.48
1954	52.0	195.6	164.7	107.7	54.3	18.1	1.3	88.3	2.97
1960	52.5	159.2	105.6	52.9	25.0	8.0	0.5	58.9	2.02
1962	46.4	143.1	94.8	47.0	20.3	6.9	0.3	52.5	1.79
1970	50.0	159.3	110.3	51.4	18.4	4.3	0.3	56.6	1.97
1973	57.5	157.0	105.1	48.1	17.9	3.9	0.2	58.2	1.95
1974	67.1	180.5	128.6	59.9	20.0	4.4	0.2	69.6	2.30
1975	72.1	183.5	133.8	62.0	20.2	4.2	0.2	72.8	2.38
1979	72.9	166.0	104.2	42.6	14.8	3.1	0.2	61.5	2.02
1980	68.0	158.6	100.0	40.9	13.7	2.9	0.1	57.6	1.92

* In the territory of Hungary prior to 1920.

Sources:
1. Klinger, 1975, p. 133.
2. Hungarian Central Statistical Office (1982), p. 127.
3. Hungarian Central Statistical Office (1976), p. 107.
4. Hungarian Central Statistical Office (1971), p. 82.
5. Hungarian Central Statistical Office (1961), p. 54.

older married females continues to decrease mainly because they do not give birth to higher parity children, i.e. third, fourth children. Thus, the reproductive period has decreased over time. The effective fertility period now ends at around the age of 35 years for most females.

Indeed, the overwhelming majority of women in Hungary, as in other industrialised countries, give birth to their children before the age of 40 (in 1960, 98.5 per cent; 99.4 per cent in 1980). Thus, the total number of births of married females aged 35-39 years can be considered as their completed family size. The percentage distribution of married women aged 35-39 by parity level, 1949-1980, illustrates the changes that have occurred in fertility (see table 1.2).

Table 1.2: Percentage distribution of married women 35-39 years by number of children, 1980

Year	Number of children						Average number of children
	0	1	2	3	4+	Total	
1949	14	21	25	16	24	100	2.53
1960	10	22	32	18	18	100	2.33
1970	7	27	42	15	9	100	2.03
1980	6	25	50	13	6	100	1.93

Source: Hungarian Central Statistical Office (1981c).

The change in Hungarian fertility is also well reflected by the changes over time in the distribution of live births by parity (see table 1.3). While at the turn of the century over one-half, and even in 1938 still 30 per cent, of the newborn were fourth and higher parity children, their proportion in 1960 was already only one-seventh and in recent years, only 5 per cent of all births. The proportion of third children scarcely changed between 1960 and 1980, whereas the proportion of first, and even more that of second children grew significantly. The mean parity decreased continuously during almost the whole period, reflecting the great changes in the distribution of births by parity.

The decrease in average parity shows that Hungarian fertility does not reach the proportion of about 40 per cent of third and higher parity children which is necessary for replacement to be attained.

The following time series of reproduction rates (see table 1.4) also reflect the change in fertility in Hungary. The net reproduction rate, which was under one during the greater part of the period after the Second World War, indicates that the Hungarian population can be expected to decrease in the period 1981-2000.

Table 1.3:   Percentage distribution of live births by parity

Year	Parity					Average of parity
	1	2	3	4+	Total	
1900	20	15	14	51	100	4.37
1938	33	22	15	30	100	3.05
1952	39	28	14	19	100	2.46
1954	35	30	16	19	100	2.50
1960	44	29	12	14	100	2.18
1962	45	29	12	14	100	2.15
1970	49	34	9	8	100	1.88
1975	44	40	11	5	100	1.87
1979	46	39	10	5	100	1.81
1980	46	39	10	5	100	1.82

Source: See table 1.1.

Table 1.4:   Reproduction rates, 1901-1979

Year (average of years)	Reproduction rate		Year	Reproduction rate	
	Gross	Net		Gross	Net
1901	2.582	1.449	1970	0.953	0.912
1910-11	2.365	1.397	1971	0.931	0.981
1921	1.828	1.128	1972	0.931	0.894
1930-31	1.385	1.010	1973	0.943	0.906
1940-41	1.194	0.972	1974	1.117	1.096
1949	1.223	1.060	1975	1.157	1.111
1950	1.259	1.106	1976	1.096	1.056
1952	1.198	1.085	1977	1.056	1.021
1954	1.428	1.312	1978	1.010	0.979
1960	0.975	0.917	1979	0.985	0.956
1962	0.868	0.817			

Sources: See table 1.1, sources 1 and 2.

Table 1.5: Comprehensive fertility indicators of Hungary, 1880–1980

Year	Live births per thousand population	Live births per thousand 15-49 year old women	Total fertility[a]	Average parity[a]	Reproduction rate Gross	Reproduction rate Net	Average no. of children of deceased married women [b]	Average no. of children born[c] of married women	Average no. of children born[c] of married women aged 50-59
1880[d]	44.4	170	5.32		2.59	1.45			
1900[d]	39.7	154	3.80	4.37	1.83	1.13	5.11	3.62	
1920	31.4	117	2.89	1.19	0.97	4.31			
1940	20.0	70							
1950	20.9	77.4	2.57	2.51	1.24	1.07		2.59	3.33
1954	23.0	88.3	2.97	2.50	1.43	1.31			
1960	14.7	58.9	2.02	2.18	0.98	0.91		2.32	2.90
1962	12.9	52.5	1.80	2.15	0.87	0.81		2.29	2.80
1970	14.7	56.6	1.96	1.88	0.95	0.91	2.65	2.01	2.42
1973	15.0	58.2	1.95	1.86	0.94	0.91	2.51	2.00	2.39
1974	17.8	69.6	2.30	1.89	1.12	1.07	2.52	1.95	2.32
1975	18.4	72.8	2.38	1.87	1.16	1.11	2.47	1.94	2.30
1976	17.5	69.9	2.26	1.84	1.10	1.06	2.42	1.94	2.28
1977	16.7	67.3	2.17	1.84	1.06	1.02	2.42	1.94	2.26
1978	15.8	64.1	2.08	1.82	1.01	0.98	2.42	1.94	2.24
1979	15.0	61.5	2.02	1.81	0.99	0.96	2.39	1.94	2.23
1980	13.9	57.6	1.92	1.82	0.94	0.91	2.34	1.89	2.14

a   On basis of the yearly calendar live birth rate.
b   From a marriage duration of 20 years or longer.
c   Population census data until 1973;   data of the continuous registration of the population for 1974-80.
d   In the territory of Hungary prior to 1920.

Sources: See table 1.1, sources 1 and 2.

1   The crude birth rate is the number of live births per thousand persons in the total population.   The general fertility rate is the number of live births per female aged 15 to 49 years.

Total fertility rate indicates the average number of children that would be born to a woman if she went through her child-bearing lifetime with age-specific fertility rates as observed in the given year.   In order for a population to replace itself, a total fertility rate of somewhat more than two is required (2.1 to 2.5 depending on mortality conditions) (Haub, 1981).

The gross reproduction rate is the average number of daughters born per woman given the age-specific fertility rates in a given year and is approximately half of the total fertility rate.

The net reproduction rate is based not only on the age-specific fertility rates but also includes the age-specific mortality rates of women.

Chapter 2

SOCIAL POLICY AND POPULATION POLICY

This chapter gives a brief survey of policies aimed at helping families with children and examines some of the effects such policies have on standard of living, female employment and fertility.

In Hungary, over 9 per cent of the net national product (according to 1980 data) was spent on social benefits and assistance related to the education of children. About one-third of it was in the form of direct financial aid given to families with children and/or to mothers. The remaining two-thirds was in the form of benefits in kind through a network of institutions (crèches, kindergartens, schools, day-time homes, students' hostels, pediatric services, etc.).

1. Financial Assistance to Families with Children

(a) Direct financial aid

Direct financial aid includes maternity benefit, pregnancy confinement benefit, child-care allowance, leave with pay to nurse a sick child, extra paid holidays for parents, and family allowance. The amount of direct financial aid grew rapidly from 1.8 per cent of the net national product in 1970, to 2.8 per cent in 1975 and 3.1 per cent in 1980. The growth in benefits can be mostly ascribed to the fact that the amounts paid as family allowance grew by 4.8 times in this period. In 1980, the amount of family allowance was 2.2 per cent of the net national product or 2.8 per cent of the national income. This is on the high side for a European socialist country; as a percentage of the national income in 1980, family allowance was 2.8 in Czechoslovakia, 2.6 in Bulgaria, 2.1 in Romania and 0.7 in Poland (documentation of the Hungarian Central Statistical Office).

Family allowance: All persons covered by social insurance (i.e. employed) are entitled to a family allowance if there are two or more children in their household who are under 16 years or over 16 years but under 19 years and attending regular primary or secondary schools, or having a chronic disease or a physical or mental abnormality.

As with other benefits, the widening of the scope of entitled persons played a great role in the increase in the amount paid as family allowance. However, the increase in the average amounts paid to the entitled persons was not as rapid as the growth in the total amount and was even less rapid if compared to earnings and to the general income situation.

The family allowance paid from July 1980 to families with two children was equal to 27.6 per cent of the average earnings, while in 1966 this proportion was 16.2 per cent.[1] The amount paid in 1980 compares well with the 21 per cent of average earnings paid in Czechoslovakia, 16 per cent in Romania, 13 per cent in Bulgaria, 9 per cent in Poland, and 4 per cent in the German

- 11 -

Democratic Republic (David and McIntyre, 1981). In the case of families with three or more children this proportion grew to 55.7 per cent, whereas in 1966 it was 27.3 per cent. At present, in the case of families with two children, the family allowance covers about 25 per cent of the average amount spent on children from the personal income of the family, and, in the case of families with three or more children, it covers about 30 per cent.

Maternity benefit: A woman is entitled to a maternity benefit if she participates in an ante-natal consultation at least once during her pregnancy and gives birth to her child during the insurance period (i.e. while employed) or within 180 days after the cessation of the insurance. Mothers are also entitled to receive a maternity benefit for stillborn children. The amount of the maternity benefit is usually 2,500 forints per child (about 70 per cent of the average monthly wage).[2]

Pregnancy confinement benefit: The pregnancy confinement benefit is payable for females who have been insured for 180 days within the two years prior to the confinement and who give birth to their children during the insurance period or within 42 days following the cessation of the insurance.

As a pregnancy confinement benefit, the total amount of the daily average income is payable for 20 weeks (in the case of an abnormal confinement this period might be lengthened by a further four weeks) if the mother has been insured for at least 270 days within two years prior to childbirth. If she has not been insured for 270 days but for at least 180 days, the amount of the pregnancy confinement benefit is equal to 65 per cent of her daily average income.

Child-care allowance: An economically active mother (employee or member of a co-operative) is entitled to a child-care allowance until the child is 3 years of age if she is on child-care leave. In the case of a multiple birth, the child-care allowance is payable for each child separately. The mother may receive an allowance for more than one child if she gives birth to a new child before the other child becomes aged 3 years.

An economically active woman has the right to the following monthly amounts of child-care allowance: 800 forints for the first child, 900 forints for the second child and 1,000 forints for the third and each further child. The allowance payable to a female member of a farmers' co-operative is 100 forints lower in each category.

A mother on child-care leave is also entitled to a bonus of 290 forints per month, independently of the number of children.

The maximum duration of the child-care allowance in Hungary is the longest of all the European socialist countries. In Czechoslovakia, the duration is until the child is aged 2, in Bulgaria until almost age one. In Poland, child-care leave (up to three years) involves no child-care allowance.

Leave with pay to nurse a sick child: Leave with pay to nurse a sick child is payable to a mother breastfeeding and/or nursing her child under 1 year of age as well as to a mother (or father living without a spouse) nursing her/his sick child under 6 years of age.

Leave with pay to nurse a sick child is payable without any limitation until the child is aged 1 year. In the case of nursing a sick child over 1 year but under 3 years, the mother or father without a spouse is entitled to leave with pay during 60 days per year for each child; if the child is over 3 years but under 6 years, the entitlement is 30 days yearly for each child (60 days in the case of a one-parent family).

Paid holidays: In addition to one free day per month without pay, the mother (or father rearing his child alone) is entitled yearly to two days' paid holiday for one child under 14 years, five days for two children under 14 years, and nine days for three or more children under 14 years.

(b) Institutions

In Hungary, there is room in crèches for about 14 per cent of children under 3 years. This relatively low proportion is related to the fact that the system of child-care allowance permits mothers to care for their children at home until the age of 3 years. This is seen as being better for the children in both health and psychological respects than care in crèches. The widening of the network of crèches is hindered by the very high costs of investment and maintenance and by their high demand on labour. Therefore, presumably the network of crèches will not be widened significantly in the near future.

There is room for nearly 90 per cent of children aged 3-5 years in kindergartens. (It is expected that this proportion will be nearly 100 per cent within a reasonable period of time.) In this age group, the education of children in a community is justified in both psychological and educational terms. This is especially important for 5 year old children as a preparation for school.

For both crèches and kindergartens, parents have to pay a certain fee based on their income. The amount of this, however, is equal to only 20-40 per cent of the total cost of the institutions; the rest is covered by the local council or enterprise maintaining the institution.

The education of 6-13 year old children at primary schools is compulsory and free of charge; enrolment is practically 100 per cent. About 40 per cent of the pupils of primary schools make use of "day-time homes", i.e. they are given lunch and remain under the supervision of teachers until the end of their parents' working day. (This is primarily for children aged 6-10 years who still need continuous supervision by adults.)

After primary school, 40 per cent of 14-17 year old children continue to study at secondary schools and a further 40 per cent of them at apprentice schools. About 10 per cent of the age group 18-23 years participate in tertiary level education (university, college). For third level education there is a fee depending on the parents' income and on the student's academic achievement. This fee, however, covers only an insignificant part of the education costs. At the same time, 80 per cent of the students receive a scholarship, almost 50 per cent of them live in students' hostels and approximately 75 per cent of them eat in canteens.

(c) Mothers' and children's health

In 1980, the infant mortality rate (number of deceased infants per 1,000 liveborn) was 23 per thousand. Infant mortality has decreased gradually, though from time to time a certain stagnation can be observed in this decline. However, the share of infant mortality in total mortality is not significant: in 1980 it was 2.3 per cent. By international comparison, however, the infant mortality level in Hungary is one of the highest among industrialised countries with a developed health system, mainly due to the rather high proportion (over 10 per cent) of premature births, i.e. newborns of less than 2,500 grams.

The majority of infant deaths occur within the first seven days following birth. In 1980, these deaths represented about 66.0 per cent of total infant deaths. Late foetal deaths and neo-natal deaths together form peri-natal deaths.[3] It is characteristic of their relative importance that in recent years peri-natal mortality has been higher than infant mortality.

The majority of the deceased infants were low-weight premature newborn infants. The lower the birth weight of the baby, the less chance it has of surviving. In 1980, newborns weighing more than 2,500 grams had a mortality rate of 8.2 per thousand while it was 152.7 per thousand for newborns weighing less than 2,500 grams. (In the case of birth weights under 1,000 grams, however, about 90.9 per cent of the infants die.)

Childhood mortality is low; in 1980 in the 1-4 year age group it was 0.6 and in the 5-9 year and 10-14 year age groups it was 0.3 per thousand. The proportion of childhood deaths in total deaths is insignificant - scarcely 0.6 per cent.

In Hungary, the health service is free of charge for citizens. Health provision is the duty of the National Health Service. The protection of mothers and infants and the health service for children form part of the integrated national health service.

Ante-natal care begins with the confirmation of pregnancy and regular examinations of the mother during her pregnancy. The examinations check the health condition of both the mother and the foetus. The health service aims to encourage ante-natal care by graduating the amount of the confinement benefit according to the frequency of the mother's participation in ante-natal consultations. Some 99.2 per cent of confinements take place in hospitals.

The health service ensures medical and preventive treatment for children until the age of 14 years. In cities, this is carried out by district pediatricians. In smaller settlements, children are treated by the district doctors who are general practitioners.

Health visitors work in the field of mothers', infants' and children's welfare. Their duty is the provision of everyday needs and they are responsible to the district pediatricians or the district doctors. Preventive medicine for pupils is the task of the school doctors.

(d) Housing rules related to population policy and their statistical impact

The population policy decrees on the allocation of dwellings and the granting of credits for home-building, formulated and adopted in 1971, and widened in 1976 and 1981, can be summarised as follows.

Socio-political preference is given for constructing and buying a dwelling to persons having a child or a dependent family member in his/her household. According to the degree of preference, the expenses of constructing or buying the dwelling are decreased by 20,000 or 30,000 forints, per child or per dependant. This reduction accordingly serves an explicit population policy purpose. The tenants of local council dwellings also have the right to such preference which would amount to a reduction of from 20-25 per cent up to a maximum of 80 per cent in the price for the dwelling according to the number of children and other family members supported by the tenant. The reduction might be granted in advance to young couples under 35 years of age still childless or with only one child.

Also, when distributing council dwellings, preference is supposed to be given to applicants with a number of children and to young couples.

The National Savings Bank grants facilities to young couples and also to families with three or more children in the payment of credit for constructing or buying a dwelling. The monthly repayment of the credit might be reduced by a maximum of 30 per cent in the first five years.

In justified cases, pre-payment of the credit might be cancelled for families of manual workers with three or more children.

For a number of years, when deciding on the applications[4] for dwellings registered with local councils, 55-58 per cent of the allocated dwellings have been given to young couples. As their proportion among the applicants for dwellings is 45-47 per cent, their chances are somewhat better than average. In spite of this, according to the data, the waiting period has not decreased for many years, i.e. the small chance of obtaining a separate dwelling still remains one of the main problems for young couples.

In the same period, the proportion of applicants for dwellings having three or more children was only about 3 per cent in the whole country, in comparison with the total number of applicants. Within two years, 37 per cent of these applications were granted. This proportion was somewhat higher in the capital (45 per cent) than in the provinces. Thus, the target of meeting the claims for dwellings for large families within two years will be reached only with some delay.

The data show that population policy decisions on dwellings have only been realised within certain limits and it is therefore difficult to state their direct effect. It can be supposed, however, that apart from obtaining a separate dwelling, the size and facilities of the dwellings exert a great influence on the attitude towards family planning of the majority of the population.

2. Effects of Social Benefits

(a) Standard of living of families with children

The above mentioned benefits have not been sufficient to reduce the great differences in income among families with different numbers of children. There have been and still are great differences in the standard of living between economically active households according to whether or not there are dependent children in the household (Hungarian Central Statistical Office, 1981e). According to data from the income surveys carried out each five-year period (1962, 1967, 1972 and 1977), the relative income situation of households with different numbers of children as compared to childless households has not improved in the last 15-20 years. This also means that the differences in absolute amounts and therefore in the ability to acquire consumer goods have grown.

The differences in the income situation of families are best reflected by the proportions between incomes per consumption unit.[5] Earlier, and also in 1977, compared to the income of families without a dependent child, the income level of families with two children (including financial benefits) was about three-quarters, that of three-child families about two-thirds, and that of families with four or more children only about one-half. The differences in income per consumption unit all have demographic reasons: in 1977, in childless active households there were only 24 dependants and inactive earners per 100 economically active persons, in households with three children there were 217, and in households with four or more children there were 314.

Households with children spend a greater share of their income on food and home-building and on the payment of credits for home-building than childless households. There is no significant difference in the proportion of clothing expenses. Of the other main consumption groups - drinks, tobacco, consumer durables of high value, household energy, the so-called "other industrial products" and services - households with children spend less both in absolute amounts and also relatively as compared to childless households.

In families with children - and particularly in large families - there are many more persons per 100 rooms than in childless families.

In respect of the supply of consumer durables, the situation is worse than average only in households with three or more children, but not in families with one child or two children. There are various reasons for this: some childless households consist of persons living alone and/or having no separate dwelling who are not always able to own consumer durables; families with one or two children acquire some of the goods before they have children; many of them receive such goods as presents from their parents.

As mentioned earlier, the family allowance covers personal expenses related to the children only to a certain extent. Differences in the per capita income between the families depend more on the number of dependants, and particularly on the number of

children than on the achievements of the workers. These differences tend to discourage families from having children.

(b) <u>Effect of the child-care allowance on
    employment and fertility</u>

Since its introduction in 1967, the child-care allowance has
exerted a great and long-lasting impact on several spheres of
socio-economic life (see Hungarian Central Statistical Office,
1981d). A brief summary follows:

(i) The child-care allowance has accelerated the increase in
female employment - especially that of young females, at least in
the legal sense. It has stimulated young women oriented mainly
towards having a family to take a job as soon as possible, as the
condition for getting the child-care allowance is employment for at
least one year. Thus, among females aged 20-29 years (including
those who are continuing their studies) employment has become
almost universal. As a consequence of this, since the end of the
1960s the fertility of economically active females - whose confinements in recent years have represented about 90 per cent of the
total number - has been higher than that of dependent females.

(ii) Due to use of the child-care allowance, from the second
half of the 1970s, on average 250,000-290,000 females have been
temporarily inactive; this represents 4-5 per cent of the total
number of employed persons, 10-12 per cent of employed females,
and over 25 per cent of employed females aged 20-29 years. The
effect of the child-care allowance is especially significant (15-18
per cent of the employed females) in those divisions of light manufacturing where the great majority of the workers are female.
The child-care allowance is used more than average by manual
workers, and among non-manual workers more by those engaged in
management.

(iii) From the point of view of the family, the overwhelming
majority of mothers with children younger than 2-3 years now
remain at home and this can be ascribed to the child-care allowance. In one-fifth of the families with a child under 15 years of
age, the mother makes use of the child-care allowance. This is
definitely favourable for the health and the psychological condition
of the child and lightens the load of the overburdened institutions
for children, in particular the crèches.

(iv) In the first period (1967-73), the demographic impact of
the child-care allowance was reflected mainly by the fact that
young women advanced the birth of their first (and to a lesser
extent of their second) children. From 1974 on, however (though
due to the larger female cohorts the number of first confinements
also increased), the impact of the child-care allowance was
reinforced by other population policy measures. Use of the
allowance increased a great deal after the second and third confinements, in particular among mothers who had earlier received a
child-care allowance for their first or second children. The
impact of the child-care allowance is also indicated by the fact that
75 per cent of females on child-care leave with their first children
plan to give birth to a further child or children.

(v) In the period 1967-80, the average amount of the allowance paid per family more than doubled. (In 1980, the average monthly amount was 1,250 forints.) This is connected, on the one hand, with the fact that it was increased twice (the second time in a differentiated way by parity) and, on the other hand, with the growth in the proportion of females (in recent years it was 10-12 per cent) receiving child-care allowance for two children at the same time. So the amount of the paid allowance increased from 1.2 thousand million forints, the 1970 value, to 3.9 thousand million forints by the year 1980 which is equal to 0.7 per cent of the national income and to 4.7 per cent of the social insurance benefits paid in money.

(vi) Use of the child-care allowance[6] has increased and at the same time it has become more similar in all socio-occupational groups. However, there are differences in the duration of use: females doing non-manual work and requiring a higher educational attainment make use of the child-care allowance for a shorter period. It can be also observed that some female manual workers return to work before the child is aged 3 years, though the average duration of use has grown continuously during the last decade (from 21 months to 23 months). The return to work earlier is sometimes hindered by the limited capacities of the crèches.

Beside the income aspects, returning to work as soon as possible is also motivated by the fact that the career of females on child-care leave is often disturbed and their social relations become weaker. This is also proved by the fact that a smaller proportion of women on child-care leave continue to study than economically active females of the same age group.

Notes

1 Persons with one child are entitled to a family allowance if they are single parents, their child has a chronic disease or a physical or mental abnormality, or he/she was previously entitled to a family allowance for two or more children but in the meantime the right for the second child has ceased, i.e. the child has reached 16-19 years of age.

Since July 1980, the amount of the family allowance has been as follows:

		Percentage of average wage
for 1 child	490 forints/month	13.8
for 2 children	980 forints/month	27.6
in case of one-parent families	1320 forints/month	37.2
for 3 children	1980 forints/month	55.7

for 4 children	2640 forints/month	74.3
for 5 children	3150 forints/month	88.7
for 6th and additional children	610 forints/child/month	

2 In 1978, the average wage in the national economy was 3,552 forints; in industry, it was 3,443 forints (CMEA, Moscow, 1979). In addition, an insuree having no right to a family allowance for one child has received a monthly bonus of 130 forints for one child since July 1979.

3 Foetal death is death prior to the complete expulsion or extraction from its mother of a product of conception, irrespective of the duration of pregnancy; the death is indicated by the fact that after such separation the foetus does not breath or show any other evidence of life, such as beating of the heart, pulsation of the umbilical cord, or definite movement of voluntary muscles. Late foetal deaths (stillbirths) are those of 28 or more completed weeks gestation.

Neo-natal death is infant death occurring after live birth but before the completion of the age of one month, at the age of 0-27 days. Within neo-natal death, infant death at the age of 0-6 days is early neo-natal death, which also represents a part of peri-natal death.

Peri-natal death comprises late foetal deaths (stillbirths) and early neonatal deaths, i.e. it includes deaths between the twenty-eighth week of pregnancy and the end of the first week after birth.

4 Application for local council dwellings is generally restricted to urban areas and low-income applicants.

5 The consumption units are:

- active earner	1.0
- children aged 0-2	0.4
- children aged 3-5	0.5
- children aged 6-10	0.6
- children aged 11-14	0.8
- dependants aged 15+ and retired persons	0.8

The calculation by consumption unit takes into consideration, on the one hand, that the needs of children are lower than the needs of adults until approximately the age of 14 years, and, on the other hand, that the so-called "common family needs" - e.g. housing, heating, etc. - are not proportional to the number of family members and so larger families can save money on these items as compared to smaller families.

6 By the term "users of the child-care allowance" we mean those females making use of the allowance out of the total number of women having had a confinement in a given year. The

frequency (proportion) of the use is the quotient of the users of the allowance and of the economically active childbearing females expressed as a percentage. Users of the child-care allowance have to be distinguished from the number of those on child-care leave which means the average number of women on child-care leave or their number at the end of the year. Their proportion to the employed in the individual socio-occupational groups is affected not only by the proportions of use after confinement but also by the duration of the use of the allowance.

Chapter 3

FEMALE EMPLOYMENT AND ITS IMPACT ON FERTILITY

1. Increase in Female Employment

In Hungary, as in some other European socialist countries, female economic activity has increased in the last three decades. This process began in the first half of the century, but was slow due to many factors; the place of women in the family, the traditional distribution of labour within the family, social habits and prejudices, the low educational attainment and qualification level of females, the relatively small number of working places corresponding to the qualifications and physical characteristics of women, etc., exerted a negative impact on female employment.

As a result of economic development, the restructuring of the national economy, and socialist industrialisation, the demand for labour increased. In particular, a relatively great number of workers left agriculture, especially in the early period, in response to the development of the other major sectors of the national economy which required a large labour force. The increased introduction of women into the labour force played an important role in meeting this demand. For this purpose, the government took measures aimed at gradually eliminating the factors impeding the growth of female employment and, through this, at the realisation of equal rights for both sexes. In almost all fields, females were given the opportunity to study and acquire a qualification and so became progressively more able to occupy posts requiring specialist knowledge. At the same time, the protection of economically active females, especially of working mothers, became institutionalised. For instance, society attempted to take over a great part of the day-time care of the children of economically active mothers.

As a result, a great choice of professions has opened up for females and gradually women have made use of this opportunity. It is true that in many cases economic factors, e.g. increase of the family income, primarily motivate females, especially married females, to take a job. But this is less and less characteristic of younger women. The changes in socio-economic life, the higher educational attainment and the general increase in cultural level have transformed women's way of thinking. Apart from the economic advantages, more and more women now choose an occupation as a vocation.

In the initial period of socio-economic transformation, the increase in economic activity rates, especially those of females, was one of the main sources of economic growth. While the demand for labour could be mostly met by males until the middle of the century, the increased demand for labour thereafter could no longer be met by males as their employment had been virtually complete for some decades.

According to data from the 1949 Population Census (which reflects the situation after the period of economic reconstruction at the end of the Second World War), there were 4,085,000 economically active persons at that time. Of these, the proportion of males was 71 per cent and that of females 29 per cent. Between 1949 and 1960, the total number of economically active persons increased by 675,000 (17 per cent), of which the growth in the number of economically active females was about half a million, which corresponded to a 42 per cent increase. Thus, during this period nearly three-quarters of the increase in the number of economically active persons resulted from the fact that many females had joined the labour force.

Between 1960 and 1980, the number of economically active persons increased by over 300,000 only because of the greater employment of females. More than 200,000 posts earlier held by males were taken by females because there were not enough men to compensate for the losses caused by retirement and death. However, the rapid increase in the number of economically active females, characteristic of the 1950 decade, lessened gradually. This can be ascribed to, among other reasons, the continuous increase in the proportion of those continuing to study, the gradual exhaustion of the female labour reserve and, in the 1970s, an ever decreasing number entering the productive age. At the same time, with the spreading coverage of the pension system and the introduction of the system of child-care allowances, the number of female inactive earners grew gradually (females on child-care leave are not categorised as economically active persons; for the period of use of the allowance they are registered as inactive earners).[1] The number of economically active females grew by 364,000 (22 per cent) in the 1960 decade and by a further 145,000 (7 per cent) in the 1970-80 period (see table 3.1).

Table 3.1:   Female population by economic activity

Year	Number (in thousands)				Economically active females as a percentage of		
	Female population	Economically active females	Inactive earners	Dependants	Total population	Economically active persons	Females of productive age
1949	4,781	1,193	125	3,463	25.0	29.2	34.6
1960	5,157	1,691	216	3,250	32.8	35.5	49.9
1970	5,318	2,055	769	2,494	38.6	41.2	63.7
1980	5,514	2,200	1,317	1,997	39.9	43.4	70.8

Source: Hungarian Central Statistical Office (1980b), tables on pp. 87 and 93.

Due to this increase, the number of economically active females at present is over one million (or about 85 per cent) higher than it was in 1949. As a result, in 1980 females represented more than 43 per cent of economically active persons while in 1949 their proportion was less than 30 per cent. In 1949, only one-quarter of the female population was economically active; but by 1980 the proportion had grown to two-fifths. If, besides this, the great number of young mothers on child-care leave, who have left work temporarily, are taken into consideration, i.e. if they are counted among the economically active females (in 1980 the number was 264,000), 45 per cent of the total female population can be considered as employed.

A more characteristic picture of the increase in the economic activity of females can be gained from studying the change in the female population of productive age (table 3.2). In Hungary females aged 15-54 years are considered as those of productive age. According to the Labour Code, children are allowed to take a job only after having completed the compulsory eight years of primary school, and the age limit for retirement is 55 years for females. Only 8 per cent of females over 55 were economically active in 1980.

In 1949, only 35 per cent and in 1960 only one-half of the females of productive age were economically active, while the proportion of dependants who did not study, i.e. the proportion of the so-called "other dependants", was high (62 per cent and 46 per cent, respectively). The share of the latter was rather significant (23 per cent) even in 1970 but after that it decreased, and in 1980 scarcely more than one-tenth (somewhat more than 300,000) of 15-54 year old females belonged to the group of "other dependants". Theoretically, this group represents the labour reserve. However, it should be taken into consideration that within this group the number of those who cannot take a job for different reasons - disease, family obligations, no possibility for local work, etc. - is significant. In addition, the unfavourable age structure of women belonging to this group hinders them from taking a job. Most of them (56 per cent) belong to the 40-54 year age group and one-quarter of them belong to the 50-54 year age group. This means that females who really want to work, and can take a job, have mostly done so.

Consequently, at present there is no significant labour reserve, even among females. In 1980, 71 per cent of females of productive age were economically active. If the significant number of young mothers having left work temporarily on child-care leave is added to this, the employment level of females aged 15-54 years is equal to 80 per cent and is not much lower than that of males (88 per cent).

In 1980, the proportion of the female population of productive age continuing to study at regular courses in secondary or tertiary level schools was 6 per cent. This group, though they are registered as dependants, cannot be equated with housekeepers because they are certain to take a job after finishing their studies, i.e. they form the basis of labour replacement. Table 3.2 presents a summary of the data cited above.

Table 3.2: Distribution of female population of productive age by economic activity (in percentages)

Economic activity	1949	1960	1970	1980
Economically active	34.6	49.9	63.7	70.8
Inactive earners	1.3	0.7	6.1	12.3
Of which on child-care leave	-	-	4.8	9.0
Dependants	64.1	49.4	30.2	16.9
Of which pupils, students	2.1	3.6	6.9	6.0
Other dependants	62.0	45.8	23.3	10.9
Total	100.0	100.0	100.0	100.0

Source: See table 3.1.

Age patterns of employment show (table 3.3) that the employment level is especially high (91 per cent) among married females aged 20-29 years. However, 31 per cent of these are on child-care leave. This is also connected with the fact that the great majority of live births also occur among mothers of this age group. Consequently, the child-care allowance contributes most of all to the decrease in the de facto economic activity of 20-29 year old women.

Table 3.3: Percentage employed of all females and of married females by childbearing age groups, 1980

Age group (years)	Economically active	On child-care leave	Total employed
All females:			
15-19	39.6	4.4	44.0
20-29	65.4	24.3	89.7
30-39	83.1	6.0	89.1
40-49	80.4	0.4	80.8
Total	71.3	10.2	81.5
Married females:			
15-19	56.2	25.5	81.7
20-29	60.1	31.0	91.1
30-39	82.1	6.8	88.9
40-49	79.5	0.3	79.8
Total	73.2	13.5	86.7

Sources: 1. See table 3.1.
2. 1980 Population Census. Detailed data based on 2 per cent representative sample (extra processing).

The employment level of married females aged 30-39 years (89 per cent) is very near that of 20-29 year old women (91 per cent) but among them the moderating impact of the child-care allowance on economic activity is less significant because among females of the age groups over 30 years the frequency of confinements decreases gradually. Four-fifths of 40-49 year old married women are employed and - except for a small proportion - are also economically active. In this age group there is no significant loss in labour force because of child-care allowances, but the share of housekeepers is higher.

2. Impact of Increased Female Employment on Fertility

The increase in female employment has influenced fertility in several ways. Overall the fertility of married women has declined. This is indicated by the number of children per 100 married females which was 257 in 1949, 232 in 1960, only 205 in 1970, and 188 in 1980. This last value - which is scarcely more than one-half of the figure for 60 years earlier - shows that at present the average number of children of married women is less than two. The value of this indicator is even lower among married females of childbearing age: in 1980, there were 171 liveborn children per 100 married females of childbearing age, while in 1949 there were 219.

On the other hand, among married women, the proportion who are economically active has increased. Thus, especially in the younger age groups, the number and proportion of babies delivered by employed mothers has increased while those delivered by dependent mothers has decreased (see table 3.4).

Table 3.4: Percentage distribution of live births by mother's economic activity status

Year	The mother is		Total
	Economically active	Dependent	
1960	33.7	66.3	100.0
1965	51.4	48.6	100.0
1970	74.5	25.5	100.0
1975	86.5	13.5	100.0
1980	88.6	11.4	100.0

Source: Hungarian Demographic Yearbooks (1960-80).

However, employed married women tend to have a smaller number of children than dependent married women. In 1980, among married females of reproductive age only 13 per cent of employed but nearly two-thirds of dependent women had three or more children. This indicates that the ever growing number of women who are economically active, an increasing proportion of whom are of childbearing age, consider the "two-child family model" as ideal. No significant change can be expected in the willingness to give birth to third and further children. Among economically active married females of reproductive age, the proportion with three children has fluctuated between 9-10 per cent since 1949, but the proportion with four or more children has decreased greatly from 9 per cent in 1949 to scarcely more than 3 per cent in 1980. Among non-working women, the proportion with four or more children has also declined since 1949. Thus, table 3.5 shows that although economically active married women have a lower fertility than dependent married women, the decline in their fertility is not more pronounced than among dependent women.

Table 3.5: Economically active and dependent married women of childbearing age by number of liveborn children (in percentages)

Year	Married women of child-bearing age	Number of liveborn children					Liveborn children per 100 married women of child-bearing age
		0	1	2	3	4 or more	
Economically active							
1949	100.0	33.7	29.1	19.5	9.0	8.7	141
1960	100.0	19.7	32.6	27.7	11.1	8.9	167
1970[a]	100.0	15.5	35.9	32.5	10.1	6.0	160
1980[a]	100.0	11.9	31.8	43.3	9.6	3.4	164
Dependent							
1949	100.0	16.1	25.2	23.7	13.9	21.1	234
1960	100.0	11.8	26.8	29.2	15.2	17.0	223
1970	100.0	7.7	24.7	36.0	16.3	15.3	226
1980	100.0	8.1	20.9	39.3	17.1	14.6	228

a Women on child-care leave are included.

Sources: 1. Hungarian Central Statistical Office (1981a), tables on pp. 44-46.
2. See table 3.3, source 2.

In 1949, the average number of children of married women aged 40-49 years - which indicates virtually the total, completed fertility - was relatively high; on average, a married woman in this age group had given birth to three children. But among economically active females the number of children was less than two even at that time. However, among women terminating the fertile period of life, economically active females still represented only a small share (14 per cent), i.e. 30 years ago the level of completed fertility was determined most of all by the relatively high number of dependent women (316 children per hundred dependent married females aged 40-49 years).

Between 1949 and 1960, while the average number of children of dependent women continuously declined, that of the economically active females increased (in 1960 there were 218 children per hundred economically active married women of 40-49 years as against 192 children in 1949).

The temporary increase in the completed fertility of economically active married females was followed by a decrease after 1960. In 1980, there were 190 liveborn children per 100 economically active married women aged 40-49 years, i.e. similar to the 1949 level. Since in 1980 four-fifths of the married women in the 40-49 age group were economically active, the fertility of the economically active category determines (almost by definition) fertility rates for all age groups. As a result of all this, on average a married women gives birth to only two children during the total reproductive period of her life as against the earlier generation when on average about three children were born during the fertile period.

Table 3.6: Number of liveborn children per hundred married women aged 40-49 years (completed fertility) by economic activity

Year	All	Economically active	Dependent
1949	298	192	316
1960	259	218	291
1970	226	209[a]	258
1980	200	190[a]	252

a Women on child-leave are included.

Sources: 1. See table 3.1
2. See table 3.3, source 2.

Thus, most of the decline in fertility is due to the lower fertility of working women and to their greater share among women of reproductive age. However, the increase in the fertility of working women between 1949 and 1960, and the absence of a marked decline thereafter, suggests that having children (a few only) is no longer an obstacle to seeking work.

At present, population reproduction depends mainly on the fertility of employed women. Thus, population policy and the related system of institutions should stimulate economically active females to be more willing than has been evident until now to give birth to and bring up second and higher parity children. For this purpose, the child-care allowance was introduced. As a consequence of this (as was indicated in Chapter 2), in the younger age groups the fertility of economically active women has become higher than that of the dependent ones. Its effect, however, is not yet evident in the data on completed fertility (of females aged 40-49 years).

3. Interdependence Between the Educational Level of Females and the Change in Fertility

The educational level of females in Hungary remained low until the 1950s. In recent decades there has been a pronounced increase in the educational level of the population, stimulated by the socio-economic transformation, and facilitated by the widening network of schools, especially at the secondary and tertiary level. Within this framework, the differences in educational attainment by sex have decreased continuously.

The educational level of females has risen much more rapidly than that of males. In the 1949-1980 period, the number of females having completed secondary school - as their highest educational attainment - increased seven times while the corresponding number of males completing the same educational level was scarcely more than three and a half times higher in 1980 than in 1949. During the same period, the number of females having completed tertiary level education grew 12 times, and that of males only three times. In 1980, 24 per cent of 18 year old and older males and 22 per cent of females of the same age had secondary or higher educational attainment as against the 9 and 4 per cent, respectively, in 1949. At the same time, the number and proportion of persons who had not completed even the 8th year of primary school decreased continuously. Among males 15 years and older in 1949, their proportion was still 78 per cent and among females it was even higher (80 per cent). These proportions decreased to 29 and 38 per cent, respectively during the three following decades. These data illustrate well the decrease of the earlier significant differences in educational level between males and females, especially in respect of secondary and tertiary level educational attainment.

The educational level of married women of childbearing age developed even more favourably than that of all females. This could also be ascribed to the fact that the aging cohorts with a lower educational level were replaced by young females of higher educational attainment.

Table 3.7: Distribution of married females of childbearing age by educational attainment (in percentages)

Educational attainment	1960	1970	1980	Index: 1980 1960 = 100.0
Primary school				
Less than 6 years	18.0	9.1	4.7	28.3
6-7 years	47.8	31.3	10.0	22.3
8 years	27.7	43.9	53.7	211.4
Completed secondary school	5.3	12.8	24.8	493.4
Completed tertiary-level school	1.2	2.9	6.8	602.4
Total	100.0	100.0	100.0	106.9

Sources: 1. Hungarian Central Statistical Office (1981a).
2. See table 3.3, source 2.

The rise in the educational level of females exerted a negative impact on fertility because women of a higher educational level give birth to fewer children (see table 3.8). The fact that less educated women (who had relatively high fertility) became a minority among married females of reproductive age contributed to the fall in fertility. The fertility of married women of reproductive age with an educational level under eight years of primary school slightly increased over two decades; in 1960 there were 231 liveborn children per 100 women and in 1980, 234 per 100 women. This fertility level is sufficient for replacement, but the share of such women and their impact on total fertility decreased rapidly. The proportion of this group among women of childbearing age decreased from 66 per cent to 15 per cent between 1960 and 1980.

Table 3.8: Number of liveborn children per 100 married women of childbearing age by educational attainment

Educational attainment	1960	1970	1980
Primary school			
Less than 6 years	282	289	306
6-7 years 212	220	224	
8 years 138	149	171	
Completed secondary school	125	113	136
Completed tertiary-level school	127	119	133
Total	198	179	171

Source: See table 3.7.

The fertility of married women of reproductive age having completed eight years of primary school also increased gradually during these two decades. However, the average number of their children was 27 per cent lower than that of females with a lower educational level. In this group in 1980, the number of liveborn children per 100 married women was 171, i.e. it corresponded to the average number of children of the total of married women of childbearing age.

In the 1960-70 period, the average number of children of females with higher educational attainment, i.e. those having completed secondary or tertiary level education, decreased. Between 1970 and 1980 it increased over the level attained 20 years earlier, but even so it was much lower than that of women of lower educational levels.

Thus, despite the fact that fertility increased somewhat during the last decade amongst women with both lower and higher educational levels, the average fertility levels themselves decreased. This decline is related to the increasing proportion of women with higher educational attainment. The depressing effect of this structural change on fertility was greater than the slight increase in fertility observed among females within the same educational level.

The increase in fertility in all the groups of females of different educational attainment is mostly due to the fact that, under the impact of the 1973 population policy measures, females advanced the date of birth of planned children. The measures affected first of all the younger females, and mainly those born in a great number in the 1950s who entered the childbearing age in the 1970s. However, among females of 40-49 years, i.e. those completing the fertile period of life, an overall decline in fertility was evident in the 1970s, irrespective of educational level.

4. Change in the Industrial and Occupational Structure of Females and its Impact on Fertility

The increase of female economic activity produced a large expansion of female employment in almost all the major divisions of the national economy. At the same time, however, the structure of the national economy changed. Between 1960 and 1980, because of redeployment from agriculture to the major non-agricultural divisions, the number of economically active females in agriculture and forestry decreased.

As a result, the composition of the industrial structure of the national economy by sex changed greatly. At present, 44 per cent of the economically active persons working in manufacturing are females as against the 23 per cent 30 years ago. Trade and services are now "feminised"; at the beginning of 1980, 63 and 60 per cent, respectively, of persons employed in these divisions were women. In these two fields, females represented the great majority of the increase (85 per cent in each) in employment after 1949; during the last three decades the number of females in these divisions grew four times and more than two times, respectively. Despite the great decrease in the number of female agriculture workers, their proportion among the economically active persons in agriculture grew after 1949 from 30 per cent to 36 per cent because the decrease in the number of male agricultural workers was even greater than that of females (three-quarters of the decrease in the total number of agricultural workers is due to the fact that males left agriculture).

Table 3.9: Proportion of economically active females among econ-omically active persons in the major divisions of national economy (in percentages)

Major division of national economy	1949	1960	1970	1980	Index:1980 1949 no. = 100
Mining & manufacturing	23.1	33.0	41.7	43.9	415.2
Building & construction	3.7	10.6	15.5	18.0	2178.0
Agriculture & forestry	29.7	38.2	38.5	36.2	52.1
Transport & communication	9.4	16.9	22.1	24.4	600.1
Trade	35.9	52.0	61.0	63.3	396.2
Water works and supply	24.1	24.4	19.3	23.2	1710.9
Non-material major divisions (of service character)	43.0	45.1	57.0	59.7	231.4
Total	29.2	35.5	41.2	43.4	184.4

Source: Hungarian Central Statistical Office (1980b), table on p. 93.

Parallel with the change in the industrial structure of the national economy, the composition of economically active persons by occupation altered greatly. The proportion of manual workers decreased gradually, and the number and proportion of non-manual workers grew rapidly.

This restructuring process affected the fertility level. The decrease in the proportion of agricultural manual workers means in practice that the group which was traditionally most fertile became less important and the group with lower fertility became more important. The fertility of the agricultural manual group was much higher than that of the other groups and was the result of the conditions and way of life of peasants. This contributed to the fact that, even in 1960, married female agricultural manual workers of reproductive age still had on average more than two children whereas, among female non-agricultural manual workers and female non-manual workers, the average was much lower than two. In consequence of the change in the living and cultural conditions of agricultural workers, the fertility of this group decreased between 1960 and 1970 and in the last decade it became almost stable at just over two children per married woman. At the same time the fertility of the two other groups increased gradually, particularly in the 1970s among non-manual workers. The main reason for this latter trend is that those females from the larger birth cohorts entering the childbearing age had their planned births more quickly.

Finally, the specific differences in fertility between the different groups remained, only their size decreased. Thus the decreasing proportion of agricultural workers meant that overall fertility of employed married females aged 15-49 years improved only moderately in the 1970s.

Table 3.10: Number of liveborn children per 100 employed married females of childbearing age by socio-economic group

Socio-economic group	1960	1970	1980
Manual workers			
In agriculture	214	209	210
In non-agricultural major divisions	156	164	172
Together	182	171	180
Non-manual workers	121	125	140
Total	167	160	164

Sources: 1. Hungarian Central Statistical Office (1981a), tables on pp. 244-247, 262-265.
2. See table 3.3, source 2.

Notes

[1] Economically active persons are those who display a gainful activity, have earnings or an income, are actually working and are employed or who have the legal status of a home-worker or member of a co-operative, i.e. who are employed at enterprises, institutions, offices, co-operatives, own-account workers or members of co-operatives. Also economically active are own-account workers, unpaid family workers, persons serving as regular soldiers and reserve soldiers if prior to their joining the army they were economically active, and persons condemned to and put in prison if before the beginning of imprisonment they already worked.

In addition, casual workers and day-labourers as well as those agricultural unpaid family workers who worked at least 90 days in the given year are considered economically active.

Also economically active are those persons who interrupt their employment to direct an economic unit, a section belonging to the socialist sector.

Inactive earners

Inactive earners are those persons who have no gainful occupation but have earnings or income. Inactive persons are:
- persons getting old-age, disability or widow's pensions, rentiers, civil-list pensioners even if they are in employment without the discontinuance of their pension;
- persons on child-care leave;
- the so-called "other" inactive earners living from leasing their land or house, from having subtenants or bedtenants or who have an income on the basis of a contract relating to support for life.

Pensioners who are in employment and therefore cease to get their pension do not belong to the group of inactive earners; they are considered as economically active persons. Nor are those persons who have a gainful occupation and beside it receive a disability or widow's pension considered inactive earners.

Dependants

Dependants are those who are neither economically active nor inactive earners because in general they have no earnings or income and they are supported by a private person or by an institution. Such persons are children under 14 years, pupils of primary and secondary schools aged 14 years or older, students of tertiary level schools (even if they are scholarship-holders), pupils of special courses, vocational schools, apprentice schools (even if they get the wages of skilled workers), home-makers and other dependants, those who look for a job the first time, dependants living on public funds, i.e. those supported by social institutions and having no earnings.

Persons of productive age

Productive age is the period from the completion of the age of 15 years to the pensionable age (for males, completed 60 years and for females, completed 55 years). Thus, persons of productive age are males aged 15-59 years and females aged 15-54 years.

Chapter 4

FERTILITY, FAMILY PLANNING AND TIME BUDGET STUDIES SINCE 1958

The diverse fertility trends in Hungary led experts to use sample survey methods to analyse the main motivations for fertility attitudes and practices. The primary aim of the studies was to learn in detail all factors relating to fertility, family planning and birth control (Klinger, 1975a, 1975b; Hungarian Central Statistical Office, 1979a, 1979b).

The series of fertility studies was begun in 1958. One part of the studies inquired into the usual topic of KAP (Knowledge - Attitude - Practice). A retrospective method,[1] common in most countries, was used. These studies were marked with three letters abbreviating the subject of the studies and were called TCS studies. (These letters are the initials of the Hungarian words: "Termékenység" = fertility, "Családtervezés" = family planning, "Születésszabályozás" = birth control.) Such studies were carried out four times in 1958, 1966, 1974 and 1977. These four studies are marked with the abbreviations TCS-58, TCS-66, TCS-74 and TCS-77, respectively.

Another Hungarian study takes a longitudinal,[2] i.e. follow-up approach to the fertility, family planning and birth control ideas and practices of individual marriage cohorts. The 1966 and later the 1974 marriage cohort were selected and observed for a long period. These studies are marked with the abbreviations HL-66 and HL-74, respectively. The abbreviations derive from the initials of the Hungarian words "Házassági Longitudinális" (longitudinal marriage study).

The couples selected from the 1966 marriage cohort were visited and interviewed in 1969, 1972, 1975 and 1980. Those selected from the 1974 marriage cohort were visited again in 1977 and at the end of 1980. On these occasions, the couples were questioned about the events, processes and changes since the last interview.

The results of these surveys relating to family planning attitudes, desired family size and birth control are given in this chapter, together with a short account of the influence of the stability of marriages on fertility.

Results from two studies of the time budget of adult women in Hungary are also included in this chapter, as they may have some bearing on fertility behaviour, especially that of economically active women.

1. Family Planning and Desired Family Size

One of the main purposes of the above-mentioned studies was to determine whether or not couples had the number of children they desired, and the extent to which family planning was being used.

The retrospective and longitudinal studies give different types of answers to the basic question - the family planning practice of women. Both types of surveys indicated that between 1958 and 1977 the number of family planners increased. In the 1958 TCS study, 63 per cent planned the number of their children at marriage. It is remarkable that in the 1966 study this proportion decreased; it was 47 per cent. However, the 81 per cent share observed in the 1977 TCS study was much higher and even surpassed the value 20 years earlier.

According to the results of the longitudinal studies, pre-marriage family planning could be observed in almost all cases; in 1966, 95 per cent, and in 1974, 98 per cent of the persons answering this question indicated a definite number of desired children. In the proportion of family planners, there were great differences by age in the earlier surveys, especially in the 1966 TCS study. The recent TCS studies, however, do not indicate a higher proportion of planners among younger females than older ones.

The number of children planned on average by females under 35 years at the date of their marriage had decreased gradually since the 1958 study; at that time it was still 2.25, but by 1966 (according to the TCS-66 study) it had fallen to 2.05 (according to the longitudinal marriage study, to 1.89). The 1974 data of persons married in 1974 showed some increase in the planned number of children. The average number of children (2.17) planned before marriage was 16 per cent higher than the number of children planned by those married eight years earlier. Similarly, the result of the 1977 TCS study indicated a somewhat increased family size planned by persons under 35 years of age as compared to the 1966 study.

These changes are due to the fact that, in comparison with 1958, the family ideal of two children became even more general. At marriage 64 per cent in 1958, 70 per cent in 1966 and 74 per cent in 1974 and 1977 of persons under 35 years of age planned two children. At the same time, the share of those desiring three or more children decreased. According to the data of the TCS-58 study, their proportion was still 22 per cent and according to the TCS-66 study, 15 per cent; in the case of persons marrying in 1966, however, it was only 9 per cent. In the 1974 marriage cohort, their proportion grew again significantly to 21 per cent. At the same time, the change in the share of those planning one child was remarkable; between 1958 and 1966 this proportion increased from 13 per cent to 20 per cent but among those married in 1974 it had fallen to 5 per cent.

The reliability and seriousness of the planning of family size is often disputed. The results of the 1974 longitudinal survey show that even before marriage the overwhelming majority (79 per cent) of the women had planned the number of their future children. Ninety-eight per cent of the brides-to-be had an idea of the number of children they wanted and 79 per cent of them had spoken to their fiancés about this. In spite of this, only somewhat more than one-half of them (54 per cent) declared that they wanted to have the indicated number of children under any circumstances. One-quarter of the women planned the number of children depending on the conditions to be expected after their marriage (housing, financial questions, studying, etc.). In total, 46 per cent of the women with plans on the size of their families indicated even before marriage that they might change their plans.

Some 98 per cent of the women who married in 1974 already had an idea of the number of their future children before marriage. The proportion of those who had also fixed the planned birth date of the children was smaller, e.g. 11 per cent of the females who had planned two or more children left the birth date of their first child to nature and 13 per cent the birth date of their second child.

An ever-growing proportion of marrying females want to give birth to their first child relatively quickly. Of the women married in 1966, 63 per cent wanted to give birth to their first child in the first two years of marriage. Among the females who married in 1974, this share had grown to 87 per cent and 54 per cent of them planned the first confinement for the first year of marriage. In view of the housing conditions at marriage this proportion seems rather high. From vital statistics it is well known that the children born in the first two years of marriage represent about 40 per cent of the live births of a given year. It is rather surprising that this is planned by the majority of females even before marriage, except for cases when pregnancy occurs before marriage.

The planned early birth of the first child is characteristic in general of marrying women, irrespective of their age, occupation, residence or educational level. Differences can be observed only in the timing within the first three years. The proportion of women planning the birth of their first child for the first year of marriage increases with their age. Similarly the share of such females is higher among manual workers, among those with a lower educational attainment and among the rural population.

The women also had a rather uniform view on the date of birth of the second child. The majority (53 per cent) thought that it would be best to give birth to the second child two years after the birth of the first child, while 22 per cent found it necessary to wait at least three years. Seventeen per cent of them, however, desired to give birth to the second child one year after the birth of the first child.

The extent to which different factors affect the timing of the birth of the first child was also asked. Of the women interviewed, 27 per cent mentioned some reason for not giving birth to a child in the first two years of marriage. The majority (60 per cent) did not know of any such reason and 13 per cent could not yet answer this question. Of the reasons, housing problems represented more than two-thirds, financial difficulties somewhat more than one-tenth, the continuation of studies 7-8 per cent and health reasons 5-6 per cent. Of the reasons indicated, studying resulted in the longest postponement of the planned birth date of the first child.

It is difficult to find a uniform and clear correlation between the planning of family size and housing conditions after marriage.

The probable reason for this is that the housing conditions immediately after marriage can be considered only as a temporary solution for the majority of young marrying persons. Their family plans, however, cover a longer period even if they are later forced to change these plans. Anyhow it can be stated that those having a separate dwelling plan a somewhat larger family than others. This, however, does not result in planning a much higher number of children than the number planned by those who begin their married life as family members in their parents' houses, as subtenants, or who temporarily live separately from one another after marriage.

It is interesting that sometimes the first children are born most rapidly to those living under the worst conditions, and that relatively few of them use contraception to prevent the early birth of the first child. This has a simple explanation; in such cases they are under pressure because of the bride's pregnancy "before time". In the 1974 survey, at the premarriage consultation (i.e. at least one month before contracting marriage), 13 per cent of the brides interviewed said they were pregnant. The data indicate that the better the housing conditions, the smaller the proportion of pregnant brides, and the worse the housing conditions, the higher this proportion.

According to the data of the study carried out eight years earlier, on the basis of the number of first completed pregnancies within eight months following the date of marriage, 20-25 per cent of the brides were pregnant at marriage. Therefore, in 1974 the proportion of pregnant brides might have been higher than was declared at the consultation, because some of those brides either denied being pregnant or were not yet aware of it.

The total number of children desired at the time of survey better indicates the changing ideas on family size than the number of children planned at marriage. According to the retrospective studies (TCS), the average of the total number of desired children decreased from 2.33 to 2.10, i.e. by 10 per cent in the 1958-66 period, decreased further only by 2 per cent, to 2.06 between 1966 and 1974 and remained on the same level in the 1974-77 period. The results of the longitudinal marriage studies thus show that the fertility trends of the recent 10-15 years on average produce around two children.

The fluctuations in the total number of children desired indicated by the different sample surveys reflects the fertility situation in Hungary during the last 20 years, including the often temporary and differential impact of the population policy measures. The effect of the introduction of the child-care allowance is markedly evident in the increase in family size plans in the 1966 longitudinal study. In the TCS studies, this impact was also reflected in the level of completed fertility between 1966 and 1974. At the beginning of the 1970s, the willingness to give birth to children weakened but it was stimulated again by the population policy measures introduced at the end of 1973. Under the impact of these measures, the average fertility level and also the average number of children desired by families increased. Young couples who married in 1974 planned on average 2.17 children for their family.   Nearly three-quarters of the families desired to have two children and one-fifth of them three children.   The share of those planning only one child was 6 per cent and there was hardly any family who wanted to remain childless.   From the differences by social groups and educational level, it could also be stated that dependent women and those with the lowest (less than six years) and with the highest educational levels wanted to have the greatest number of children.

A significant number of females belonging to the 1966 marriage cohort were affected by the 1973 population policy measures just at the time when they had to decide upon the birth of their third children.   The fact that the proportion of women desiring three or more children more than doubled as compared to their ideas at marriage can probably be ascribed to the effect of the measures taken.   However, this 20 per cent in 1980 is still not sufficient for the replacement of the population and it is much lower than the proportion of families with three or more children envisaged by the population policy measures.   On average, 2.30 children per family are needed for replacement.   This average number of children was last attained by the women who are now over 60 years of age, i.e. those who were in their childbearing period in the 1940s and 1950s.   The average number of children of the female cohorts having completed their fertility since then has been lower than the replacement level.   Married women of 45-49 years at present have only two children on average.

Propaganda encouraging the three-child family ideal first affected the young people married in 1974.   At their marriage, 19 per cent of them desired/planned three children for their future family.   This was the highest proportion stated in the family planning studies to date.   In the next three years, however, this proportion decreased.   The proportion desiring one child grew more than 2.5 times (from 6 per cent to 17 per cent) while the proportion planning three children fell from 20 per cent to 13 per cent.   In the following three years, presumably due to the fact that the family allowance was increased several times and in a differentiated way, the proportion of females desiring three children did not continue to decrease and in 1980 it was still 13 per cent.   However, if the stated 1980 plans were realised, only families of the lowest educational level would have as many children as are necessary for the replacement of population.

For the great majority (76.1 per cent) of females, the originally planned family size did not change between 1974 when they married and 1980.   Some 17.2 per cent of females desired fewer children than before marriage (8.6 per cent of women desired two children instead of the original three and 6.3 per cent wanted one child instead of the original two).   Only 6.7 per cent wanted to have more children, 3.7 per cent desiring three children instead of two and 2.2 per cent wanting two children instead of the one planned originally.

In the 1980 longitudinal study, it was found that there was a much greater difference in the number of desired children by age of female in the sixth year of marriage than at the date of marriage.   The desired number of children of women marrying for the first time or remarrying at over 25 years of age was much lower than their original ideas at marriage. A decrease could also be observed, though to a smaller extent, among those marrying at under 25 years of age. In the sixth year of marriage, the youngest females wanted to have the greatest number of children, but on average only somewhat more than two children. At marriage (in 1974), the 25-29 year old females desired the most children, on average 2.20.

The population policy measures affected females differently according to socio-occupational status, residence and educational level. This is reflected in the desired family size and its realisation, as well as in the number of living children. Third children were born mainly in families in the rural population and of agricultural manual occupation. Among females living in the capital and other urban areas in 1975, the proportion of families with three and more children was only one-half that of rural families. This proportion was four times as high among agricultural manual workers as among non-manual workers.

In 1980, also, the only social group in which the planned number of children had not fallen was that of agricultural manual workers (see table 4.1) who by then desired the greatest number of children (2.21). The decline was the greatest among non-manual workers. In 1980, their planned number of children did not even reach 1.9, with only 10 per cent wanting three or more children (as compared to 22 per cent at marriage), and the proportion of those desiring one child quadrupled (from 5 per cent to 20 per cent). It is characteristic of all the occupational groups that the proportion of females planning three children decreased to the extent that the proportion of women desiring one child grew; the proportion of those planning two children showed only slight fluctuations.

The decrease was smaller among dependent females than among economically active ones. Among the former, the proportion desiring three or more children was still twice as high as among economically active females. There were also great differences in 1980 by residence of females as compared to six years earlier at marriage. There was a sharp decline in the planned number of children of women living in the capital. The percentage desiring one child nearly tripled to about 23 per cent and the percentage planning three children fell from 20 to 12 per cent.

The total number of children desired also declined differently depending on the female's educational level. Among those having completed university or college, the proportion desiring one child tripled, but the proportion planning three and more children fell from 35 per cent to 22 per cent between 1977 and 1980. (However, it is still higher than the value stated in the earlier longitudinal studies.)

It is difficult to find an exact relation between family income and the desired number of children (table 4.2). The income of females divorced or living separately was lower than that of women living with their husbands. For this reason the smallest average number of planned children (about 1.7) occurred in the two lowest

- 40 -

income categories. For families in the higher income categories, a uniform relationship cannot be stated as all income groups planned about 2.0 children. However, in the highest income categories, plans relating to number of children showed a greater spread. In this group, the number of those planning three children and planning one child was the greatest; therefore, the share of families desiring two children was below the average.

Table 4.1: Number of children planned at marriage (1974) and in the sixth year of marriage (1980) by socio-occupational group and residence (in percentages)

	Planned number of children					Total	Aver-age
	0	1	2	3	4+		
Occupational groups							
Economically active Agricultural manual workers							
1974	0.5	5.6	74.7	16.7	2.5	100.0	2.15
1980	1.3	9.4	61.0	23.9	4.4	100.0	2.21
Non-agricultural manual workers							
1974	0.0	6.1	75.7	16.7	1.5	100.0	2.14
1980	1.1	15.4	66.9	14.4	2.2	100.0	2.01
Non-manual workers							
1974	0.2	4.9	73.1	20.1	1.7	100.0	2.18
1980	1.4	19.4	68.9	9.6	0.7	100.0	1.89
Dependants							
1974	0.2	4.9	73.1	20.1	1.7	100.0	2.18
1980	1.4	19.4	68.9	9.6	0.7	100.0	1.89
Residence							
Budapest							
1974	0.0	7.6	68.8	20.2	3.4	100.0	2.19
1980	1.9	22.3	62.0	12.2	1.6	100.0	1.89
Other urban areas							
1974	0.1	5.8	73.3	19.4	1.4	100.0	2.16
1980	1.2	16.6	68.4	12.2	1.6	100.0	1.96
Rural areas							
1974	0.2	5.1	74.3	18.6	1.8	100.0	2.17
1980	1.0	14.6	68.3	14.1	2.0	100.0	2.02

Source: Hungarian Central Statistical Office (1979b).

At present it seems that fertility sufficient for replacement is planned only by female agricultural manual workers, and by those who have not completed eight years of schooling. Because of social and regional mobility and the increase in the general socio-economic level, the proportion of these groups within the total population is decreasing, and this may contribute to a still further decline in fertility.

2. Birth Control

The decline in the Hungarian birth rate and in fertility observed since the end of the last century is due in part to the gradual spread of birth control. Until the second half of the 1960s, pregnancy was prevented mostly by the so-called traditional methods: coitus interruptus, rhythm method and vaginal douching. Some mechanical methods were also used, mainly the condom and pessary and, to a lesser extent, chemical contraceptives.

Table 4.2: Average number of desired children of females married in 1974, six years after marriage, by the total income of the family, 1980

Income categories (Ft)	Average number of desired children
Less than 2,999	1.70
3,000-3,999	1.78
4,000-4,999	2.14
5,000-5,999	1.97
6,000-6,999	2.03
7,000-7,999	2.06
8,000-8,999	2.03
9,000-9,999	2.02
10,000-10,999	2.01
11,000 and more	2.05[a]
Total	2.01

a 2 per cent of sample.

Source: Provisional data not yet published of the 1980 follow-up survey of persons married in 1974.

Until the middle of the 1950s, undesired pregnancy could be legally terminated only if the health or life of the pregnant woman or her future child were endangered. For some decades, the hospitals and clinics of Hungary were obliged to report on abortions. · In the second half of the 1940s, and in the first half of the 1950s, the yearly number of reported abortions was very low (a maximum of 2,000-3,000). According to various estimates, however, until 1956 about 100,000-150,000 illegal abortions were carried out yearly in Hungary, often under very poor sanitary conditions which had a harmful effect on the health of females and in many cases even endangered the birth of children desired later. From the second half of the 1950s, several health measures were taken in Hungary relating to birth control, e.g. in mid-1956 a decree legalised and facilitated the termination of undesired pregnancies. One of the purposes of the legalisation was to avoid the harm done to health by illegal abortions. But in addition, both the government and public opinion concurred that all females had the right to decide on the number of their future children and thus to use this method of birth control. The authorisation of abortion was also motivated by the fact that at that time in Hungary family planning and the availability of modern contraceptives were in their initial stages.

Table 4.3: Number and ratio of abortions

Year	No. of abortions (1000)	Abortions	
		per 1000 females aged 15-49	per 100 live births
1950	1.7	0.7	0.9
1960	162.2	65.1	110.7
1970	192.3	71.5	126.7
1973	169.7	63.3	108.6
1974	102.0	38.1	54.8
1975	96.2	36.1	49.5
1976	94.7	35.7	51.1
1977	89.1	33.8	50.2
1978	83.5	31.9	49.7
1979	80.8	31.0	50.4
1980	80.9	31.4	54.4

Source: Hungarian Central Statistical Office (1982).

In 1958, after the legalisation of abortion, 146,000 induced abortions were reported by the hospitals and clinics carrying out these operations. The number of cases grew almost continuously in the following years until 1969. In that year, statistics covering all cases registered almost 207,000 terminations of pregnancy. In 1969, there were 134 terminations of pregnancy per 100 live births, whereas in 1958 this value had been 92. After 1969, a small decline began due to the spread of modern contraceptives. In 1973, despite the decrease, the number of induced abortions was still higher than the number of births.

A significant decline occurred in 1974 when the number of abortions fell by 40 per cent to 102,000. Two measures played a significant role in this great decrease. From October 1973, the

purchase of oral contraceptives became easier.   The other reason
was that, in order to protect the health of females and of their
future children, the decree authorising abortions was made more
restrictive.[3]   From 1974 on, the number of abortions continued
to decrease moderately.   In 1980, 81,000 cases were reported;
there were 54 induced abortions per 100 live births.   By international comparison, this proportion can be considered as average.
    The above-mentioned trends are also reflected in the sample
surveys.   The proportion of married women having had an
induced abortion decreased from 55 per cent to 44 per cent in the
1958-1977 period.
    The legalisation of abortion contributed to the low number and
rate of births in Hungary.   It should be emphasised, however,
that in Hungary a negative correlation between abortions and the
number of births existed only until the end of the 1960s.   In the
second half of the 1960s, the number of births and the number of
abortions grew in parallel.   After 1970, there was a continuous
decrease in the number of induced abortions;   at the same time the
number of births grew until 1975.   Since then the birth rate has
declined simultaneously with the number of induced abortions.
    Our sample surveys also dealt with the attitude of females to
birth control.   Table 4.4 shows the change in contraceptive
practice of 15-39 year old married women in the last 20 years.

Table 4.4:   Percentage distribution of 15-39 year old married
women by birth control methods, 1958, 1966, 1977

Study	Method to control the number of their births			Do not use birth control	Sterile	No. of women
	contra- ception only	abortion only	both methods			
TCS-58	21	17	37		25	5,641
TCS-66	32	10	42	13	3	6,094
TCS-77	52	3	30	12	3	4,009

Sources: 1.   Hungarian Central Statistical Office (1963), p. 44.
          2.   Demographic   Research   Institute   (1970-75),   pp.
               148-149.
          3.   Hungarian Central Statistical Office (1980a), p. 11.

    There was a great improvement in birth control practices.
This improvement is shown by the fact that at the end of the
1950s, among married women under 40 years of age, one-fifth used
contraception to control the number of their confinements, while in
1977 over one-half of women did so.   Also, the proportion of
women using only induced abortion for birth control decreased.

Table 4.5: Practice of contraception at present among married women aged 39 years and younger, 1958, 1966, 1977 (in percentages)

	1958	1966	1977
Users of contraception	59	68	73
Non-users of contraception	41	32	27
Total	100	100	100

Sources: 1. See table 4.4, source 1.
2. Hungarian Central Statistical Office (1980a), p. 29.

Nevertheless, the proportion of women combining abortion with other methods was high (30 per cent) even in 1977. The reason for this was that a great proportion of women using contraception used inefficient methods or did not use contraception regularly. This statement, however, does not contradict the fact that the contraceptive practice of married women expanded rather rapidly. (The sale of the first hormonal contraceptive pill began in 1967 and the use of the IUD also began at that time.) In the last two decades an ever-growing proportion of married women have controlled fertility with some contraceptive method.

Every year an almost equal proportion (15-16 per cent) of females did not use contraception because they were pregnant, they desired to give birth to the next child or they were sterile. Thus, between 1958 and 1977 the share of married women who did not use contraception for other less acceptable reasons decreased from 25 per cent to about 11 per cent.

At the same time, particularly between 1966 and 1977, a change also occurred in the type of contraceptive methods used, as can be seen in table 4.6.

There is a strong positive correlation between the use of contraceptive methods and the duration of marriage. In present Hungarian practice, the great majority of women give birth to their first child in the first years of marriage; therefore, the proportion of females using contraception in this period is relatively low. Only one-third of the women covered by the 1966 longitudinal marriage study used contraception in the period immediately after marriage (table 4.7). In three years (from 1966 to 1969), the share of users more than doubled which shows that contraception becomes general only after the birth of the first child. In the following period, the proportion of users continued to increase more moderately; at a six-year duration of marriage the share of those using some contraceptive method was 73 per cent and at a nine-year duration of marriage it was 75 per cent among females under 45 years of age.

Table 4.6: Percentage distribution of married women aged 39 years and younger using contraception, by main methods used, 1958, 1966, 1977[a]

Main method of contraception	1958	1966	1977
Coitus interruptus	52.3	63.0	23.4
Other natural methods	15.0	9.1	5.2
Condom	21.2	17.5	5.9
IUD	-	0.1	13.1
Other mechanical methods	4.8	5.9	1.1
Oral pills	-	0.2	49.3
Other methods	6.7	4.2	2.0
Total	100.0	100.0	100.0

a According to the data of the 1958, 1966 and 1977 fertility, family planning and birth control studies.

Sources: 1. See table 4.4, source 1.
2. See table 4.5, source 2.

Table 4.7: Percentage distribution of female users by main method of contraception in the 1966 marriage cohort

Main method of contraception	Date of interview			
	1966	1969	1972	1975
Natural	65.5	50.1	42.0	31.0
Mechanical	21.0	16.9	16.9	19.3
Chemical	5.2	3.5	1.8	1.3
Oral	4.2	24.3	35.8	47.3
Other	4.1	5.2	3.5	1.1
Total	100.0	100.0	100.0	100.0
Of 100 women:				
users	31.3	66.5	72.9	74.7
non-users	68.7	33.5	27.1	25.3

Source: Hungarian Central Statistical Office (1979b).

The methods which are used and the efficiency of those methods are also important questions. A great change occurred in the 1966-75 period with the growing importance of oral contraceptives. The first oral contraceptive became available in pharmacies in 1967, i.e. in the first year of marriage of the women covered by the survey. Later, the prescription of oral pills became more frequent and other types also became available. Thus, the spread of oral contraceptives and the declining use of natural methods (coitus interruptus, the rhythm method or their combination) can be seen in the practice of the 1967 marriage cohort.

Use of modern, efficient contraceptive methods was related to age. The use of oral contraceptives spread most rapidly among young married women. In 1975, it was generally characteristic of women under 30 years of age that, after nine years of marriage, a much greater proportion of them used oral contraceptives than natural methods, and one-half of those using mechanical methods used the IUD.

Among women over 30 years of age, the natural contraceptive methods were still the most popular. Of them, coitus interruptus was widely used, and the husbands of women of this age used the condom more frequently. Oral contraceptives also became popular among persons aged 30-35 years, but many females over this age went back to a natural contraceptive method even though they might have tried oral contraceptives at some time (see table 4.8).

Table 4.8: Main method of contraception among users in the 1966 marriage cohort by age groups (in percentages)

Age group on 1.1.1973	Natural	Mechanical	Chemical	Oral	Other
20-25					
1969	51.4	15.5	3.4	26.4	3.3
1972	41.2	13.0	1.7	41.8	2.3
1975	27.3	17.3	0.5	54.3	0.6
26-30					
1969	46.8	18.3	4.0	25.6	5.3
1972	39.3	18.7	2.4	36.5	3.1
1975	30.7	19.8	1.7	46.6	1.2
31-35					
1969	56.5	16.4	2.5	17.7	6.9
1972	46.7	18.9	0.9	27.7	5.8
1975	40.9	23.9	1.0	32.2	2.0
36-40					
1969	56.3	11.5	2.3	19.5	10.4
1972	51.7	16.9	3.3	14.6	13.5
1975	60.3	14.7	1.5	20.6	2.9

Source: See table 4.6.

At the start, the use of oral pills became popular mainly among urban females and those of a non-manual occupation. The social differences in this respect observed in 1969 decreased greatly after three years and had ceased by 1975. Thus, oral contraceptives were used equally by women living in the capital or in the country, as well as by those of different social groups and occupations. This was not true for the users of natural and mechanical contraceptive methods, though the differences decreased greatly in the 1969-75 period. Natural contraceptive methods were always used more frequently by rural women than by urban ones, and they were more popular among manual workers than among non-manual workers.

3.   Stability of Marriages

As the stability of marriages may have some influence on fertility levels, the findings on that subject from the 1980 longitudinal survey are given here.

On the basis of divorce statistics, the stability of marriages can be stated only indirectly because deteriorating conjugal relations do not always result in the legal dissolution of marriage or may produce a divorce only after a certain time. The sources of conflict in family life, their frequency and impact, and the real or supposed causes of divorce can be stated only by means of sample surveys.

For many years, Hungary has had high divorce rates. At present there is one divorce per three marriages. If the 1980 age-specific divorce rates starting from the average age of females marrying for the first time (21 years) remained stable for a long period, 25 per cent of marriages would end with divorce before the woman reached the age of 35 years and more than one-third by the end of the female's childbearing age.

The longitudinal marriage surveys present the incidence of divorces of the individual marriage cohorts by duration of marriage. Six years after marriage, 10.8 per cent, and 10 years after marriage, somewhat more than 14 per cent of the women married in 1966 were divorced.

In the 1980 survey of females who had married five and a half years earlier, i.e. in 1974, 7.1 per cent were divorced (table 4.9). This indicates a decline in the divorce rates of this cohort. This might be partly ascribed to the fact that only females under 35 years were included in the 1974 sample, i.e. the age structure of the sample is younger than that of the 1966 cohort. (Older women divorce more frequently than younger ones. This is confirmed by the data of both longitudinal marriage surveys.)

The incidence of separation is somewhat different by age. The ratio of women legally married but living separately from their husbands was somewhat higher in the youngest age group (20-24 year old) and was lower in the oldest age group (36-40 year old).

Altogether, 90 per cent of the women still lived with the husbands they had married five years earlier. This proportion, however, differs according to female residence and occupation. A higher incidence of divorce is associated with female economic activity and economic independence. The divorce rate is much lower among dependent females. Among economically active women, those with a non-manual occupation have the highest and agricultural manual workers have the lowest divorce rates. The attitude of females living in the capital differs greatly from the attitude of women living in other areas. Within five years, nearly 11 per cent of marriages contracted in Budapest ended in divorce, and here also separation was most frequent. Thus, in Budapest at the end of 1980, only 85 per cent of the women still lived with the husbands they had married five years earlier. Among rural females this proportion was nearly 93 per cent.

Table 4.9: Percentage distribution of females married in 1974 by marital status, socio-occupational group, residence and number of children in 1980

| | Marital status | | | | | |
| | Married | | Widowed | Divorced | | Total |
	living with husband	living separately from husband		living with a partner	living alone	
Occupation						
Economically active	90.2	1.6	0.8	1.2	6.2	100.0
Non-agricultural manual workers	90.3	1.8	0.6	1.7	5.6	100.0
Agricultural manual workers	89.9	4.4	0.0	1.3	4.4	100.0
Non-manual workers	90.0	1.2	1.0	0.7	7.1	100.0
Dependants	94.8	2.8	0.7	0.7	1.0	100.0
Residence						
Budapest	85.3	3.1	0.8	1.5	9.3	100.0
Other urban areas	90.2	1.1	0.9	1.5	6.3	100.0
Rural areas	92.8	1.6	0.7	0.8	4.1	100.0
Total	90.4	1.7	0.8	1.2	5.9	100.0
Number of children						
Living	1.62	1.52	1.31	1.38	1.04	1.58
Planned at present[a]	2.01	1.85	1.83	1.98	1.50	1.97

[a] Sum of the average number of living children and additional children desired.

Source: Provisional data not yet published of the 1980 follow-up survey of persons married in 1974.

Naturally, the stability of marriage greatly affects family size, i.e. the number of children. Five years after marriage, over 50 per cent of the married women living with their husband had two living children and one-third of them had one living child. The proportion of three-child females was the same as that of childless ones (5.8 per cent). Thus, these females had on average 1.62 living children; divorced women, however, had on average only 1.10 children.

The average number of children of couples living together without marriage is lower than that of married couples; however, it is higher than that of females divorced and living alone. The total number of desired children is equal among married couples and couples living together without marriage. This means that the female partners in life, accepting this status or hoping to get married later, desire on average the same number of children as married women who live with their husband. This is interesting because until now it could only be stated that, in the case of remarrying females, divorce and remarriage did not always mean a smaller completed family size; it was not possible to comment on partners living together. No doubt, however, in this latter group of females there are more factors of uncertainty regarding the realisation of their plans.

The proportion of marriages ending in divorce and that of persons living separately are only one indicator of the stability of marriages. Interviews with persons married in 1966 gave further information suggesting that three years after marriage more than 30 per cent of females had been disappointed by it and thought that it would have been better not to marry. At a marriage duration of six years, this proportion reached 38 per cent. In addition, of the females married in 1974 and living in marriage in 1980, 14 per cent declared that they had already experienced a critical period which seriously endangered their marriage. This proportion was above average among the youngest and oldest women and somewhat higher among dependent than among economically active women. In Budapest, not only was the proportion of actual divorces the highest but also the proportion of marriages which had survived a critical period was over 18 per cent. The relation between the number of living children and the stability of existing marriages is characterised by the fact that, in the case of three or more children, more family conflicts, even conflicts which seriously endanger their marriage, are lived through by the spouses without divorce. In the case of fewer children, however, the number of divorces is higher.

What are the causes of marriage crises and what are the most frequent reasons for marriages breaking up? Those interviewed were asked to choose and rank four of the twelve reasons given in the survey. The females divorced at the date of the survey or earlier indicated the reasons for their divorce retrospectively; the women who were married at the date of the survey, however, could also indicate the reasons jeopardising their present relationship.

There were some differences in the distribution of reasons indicated for previous divorces and for problems in the existing

Table 4.10: Causes of divorces and causes jeopardising existing marriages by female socio-occupational group (in percentages)

Occupation	Causes indicated primarily										
	Financial	Emotional alienation	Jealousy	Alcohol	Rough treatment	Extramarital sexual relation	Conflicts with parents	Conflicts relating to the child's education	Neglect of family	Other	Total
Previous divorce											
1. Economically active	6.2	25.4	4.4	24.1	8.5	8.3	7.2	0.8	6.3	8.8	100.0
2. Agricultural manual workers	0.0	11.6	0.0	42.3	11.5	3.8	7.7	3.8	7.7	11.6	100.0
3. Non-agricultural manual workers	6.0	21.9	5.2	27.4	9.7	9.2	4.7	0.5	6.5	8.9	100.0
4. Non-manual workers	6.8	29.7	3.8	19.4	7.6	7.6	9.8	0.8	6.0	8.5	100.0
5. Dependants	6.5	19.3	6.5	19.3	12.9	16.1	9.7	0.0	0.0	9.7	100.0
Total	6.2	25.0	4.5	23.9	8.9	8.6	7.3	0.7	6.1	8.8	100.0
Existing marriage											
1. Economically active	14.3	15.8	8.9	16.8	2.5	6.7	15.0	2.7	7.8	9.5	100.0
2. Agricultural manual workers	6.3	0.0	31.1	25.0	12.5	0.0	6.3	0.0	6.3	12.5	100.0
3. Non-agricultural manual workers	15.8	15.0	9.2	23.3	3.3	6.6	10.3	1.1	7.0	8.4	100.0
4. Non-manual workers	13.1	17.7	7.2	8.9	0.8	7.2	21.0	4.6	8.9	10.6	100.0
5. Dependants	17.9	7.7	10.3	25.6	2.6	10.3	20.5	0.0	5.1	0.0	100.0
Total	14.5	15.3	9.0	17.5	2.5	6.9	15.3	2.5	7.6	8.9	100.0

Source: Provisional data not yet published of the 1980 follow-up survey of persons married in 1974.

marriages. In the case of one-quarter of marriages which ended with divorce, emotional alienation and lack of affection and understanding contributed to divorce, but the excessive consumption of alcohol by the spouse was mentioned almost as frequently. Alienation and alcohol consumption were combined, on the one hand, with rough treatment and, on the other hand, with extramarital sexual relationships. About 17-18 per cent of the divorces can be ascribed to the two latter reasons. After this, conflicts with the husband's parents are mentioned most frequently (7 per cent), followed by neglect of the family and by problems of a financial character (6 per cent each).

As for the reasons jeopardising existing marriages (on the basis of the responses of females having indicated such reasons), the excessive consumption of alcohol by the spouse was mentioned most often (18 per cent). It was followed by conflicts with the mother-in-law, father-in-law or parents and by emotional alienation in an equal proportion (15 per cent each). The stability of existing marriages was also greatly endangered by financial problems and by jealousy. It should be mentioned that the questionnaire did not ask which spouse originated the causes jeopardising marriage or contributing to divorce, but the questions were put to the women.

The reasons indicated differ according to the women's age, occupation, residence or educational level. The excessive consumption of alcohol by the husband was mentioned in the first place by the youngest females, manual workers and dependants in a greater number than average. Also, in rural families and among those with the lowest educational level, the excessive consumption of alcohol was observed more frequently than average. In the case of female non-manual workers, relations with parents, mothers-in-law, or fathers-in-law jeopardised the stability of marriage most of all.

This reason was more frequent in the capital than in rural areas probably because of the necessity of living together, i.e. in the same flat. Emotional alienation increased in parallel with the education level and it was the most important reason endangering marriage among women with the highest educational level. Financial difficulties were mentioned most frequently by dependent females and those living in the capital as well as, somewhat surprisingly, by the women with tertiary level education. Jealousy was indicated more frequently than average by rural females, those of manual occupation and with the lowest educational level.

Women who mentioned a reason which seriously endangered their marriage had on average more children than those who did not indicate such a reason. Those women who mentioned the husband's alcohol consumption, rough treatment, neglect of the family and financial problems had the most children, while those who referred to emotional, psychological problems or conflicts with relatives had far fewer children than average.

4.   Time Budget of Adult Women in Hungary

Two surveys of the time budget of adult women are available in Hungary (Hungarian Central Statistical Office, 1965, 1981b). The first survey was performed in 1963, the second in 1976-77. The first covered one month (March), the second an entire year. The first used a representative sample of the population aged 18-60 years, not engaged in regular education. The second used a sample of the population aged 15-69 years.

In the analysis of changes in the time budget from 1963 to 1976-77, the sample of the survey of 1976-77 was matched to that of the survey of 1963; only the time budgets of persons aged 18-60 years not in regular education (i.e. not students) and only the time budget in the months from December to May (i.e. March and the neighbouring months) were taken into consideration. However, in the analysis of the situation in 1976-77, the time budgets of the complete sample from that year (November 1976 to October 1977) were used, i.e. all persons aged 15-69.

The time budgets of employed women and of inactive earners and dependent women were analysed separately, because of the important differences between the two groups. The time budgets of employed men are also given for comparison.

With respect to changes in the time budget (see table 4.11), it should first be noted that after 1963 the employment of women increased. In 1963, 53 per cent of the women aged 15-54 years were active earners, while in 1980 this percentage was 70.8 per cent. The growing economic activity of women was an important factor in the changes of their time budgets.

The main changes in the time budgets of women were as follows:

1.   The time spent in earning activities, i.e. working in the main job, increased on average for women, because of the increasing proportion of women in economic activity. However the regular working time of employed women (as well as that of employed men) declined.

2.   Farming activities around the household in rural areas remained an important item in the time budget of women living in rural areas. These agricultural activities provide an important additional source of income for these families. Men, however, increased their working time in these household plots after 1963, so that in 1976-77 they spent more time than women in this field.

3.   Time spent by women in transport also increased, partly in consequence of their economic activity, but also because transport times increased slightly for every adult (as a result of increasing commuting).

4.   Time spent in household chores diminished for all women, but only slightly for employed women.

5.   The building of houses and different do-it-yourself repair work were important items in the daily time budget of men, but much less so in that of women. However, the time input

Table 4.11: Time budget of economically active men aged 18-60 and of economically active and inactive women aged 18-60, in 1963 and in 1976-77 (in minutes per day)

Activity	Economically active men		Economically active women		Economically inactive women		All women	
	1963	1976-77	1963	1976-77	1963	1976-77	1963	1976-77
Earning activities	432	345	324	289	18	34	162	203
Household farming	24	45	24	22	60	79	42	42
Transport	66	75	48	62	0	40	24	55
Household chores	42	39	210	206	396	309	312	242
Building and repairing in the household	18	38	6	9	12	16	6	11
Caring for children	12	15	30	25	54	48	48	33
Other obligatory activities	18	9	18	7	24	8	18	7
Leisure	174	224	144	178	168	207	156	188
Passive rest	18	21	12	15	18	30	18	20
Sleep and other physiological needs	636	629	624	627	690	669	654	639
Total	1440	1440	1440	1440	1440	1440	1440	1440

Sources: 1. Hungarian Central Statistical Office (1965), p. 155.
2. Hungarian Central Statistical Office (1981b), p. 795.

of women in these activities also increased.

6. Time spent in the care of children by women somewhat diminished after 1963.

7. Leisure time for both active and inactive women increased after 1963. Most of the increased leisure time was spent in viewing television programmes.

With respect to the time budget of women aged 15-69 years in 1976-77, as compared to that of men, it can be stated that women work longer hours than men. The total time spent in different "duties" (earning, household farming, transport, household chores, building and repairing the household, child-care) was as follows:

	Hours/minutes per day
all men aged 15-69	8 hours 31 minutes
all women aged 15-69	9 hours 27 minutes
economically active men	9 hours 35 minutes
economically active women	10 hours 34 minutes

The work of economically active women was especially great, as their total time spent in "duties" was one hour longer than that of economically active men.

Table 4.12: Time budget of all men and women aged 15-69 and of economically active men and women aged 15-69, in 1976-77 (in minutes per day)

Activity	All		Economically active	
	Men	Women	Men	Women
Earning activities	279	171	341	259
Household farming	64	53	58	50
Transport	74	56	77	72
Household chores	64	256	60	226
Building and repairing in the household	28	5	26	5
Caring for children	12	26	13	22
Learning, culture, entertainment	253	202	222	171
Sleeping	496	512	482	488
Other physiological needs	170	159	161	147
Total	1440	1440	1440	1440

Source: See table 4.11, source 2.

The longer hours worked by women are primarily the consequence of the unequal distribution of household chores. Although men performed a somewhat increasing proportion of these household chores, and although the time spent on household chores by women diminished in consequence of the mechanisation of housework and of better commercial shopping possibilities, women still performed the overwhelming part of household chores.

Marital status and number of children were factors that differentiated the time budget of women rather strongly. Table 4.13 shows the two activities that were most clearly differentiated from this point of view, namely household chores and care for children.

Thus, the time left for leisure was shorter for women than for men. In consequence, women read somewhat less (in the case of book reading the difference was not significant; the reading of newspapers and periodicals, was, however, much more frequent among men), they viewed somewhat less television, and they spent less time in socialising, in sporting activities and in most other leisure activities.

Table 4.13: Effect of marital status and number of children on women time budget (in minutes)

| | Average daily time spent in | |
	household chores	caring for children
Single	205	10
Married, no children	300	14
Married with one child	288	33
Married with two or more children	313	62
Divorced and widowed with child(ren)	234	33

Source: See table 4.11, source 2.

The total time spent in "duties" by economically active women may partly influence their fertility patterns. The time budget surveys did not include fertility attitude questions; however, the unequal distribution of household duties between wife and husband could induce, in the case of working women, psychological effects which may negatively influence their fertility behaviour.

Notes

1　A detailed description of methodology can be found in Chapter 5.

2　A detailed description of methodology can be found in the Appendix.

3　According to the 1956 Decree the interruption of pregnancy was authorised on request if the duration of pregnancy was not longer than 12 weeks. The 1973 modification of the decree made some restrictions. Interruption of pregnancy is authorised:

(a) if the pregnant female is not younger than 35 years;
(b) if she has three or more children or had three confinements/ pregnancies;
(c) if the pregnancy resulted from rape;
(d) if the woman is not married;
(e) if it is medically justified/ for medical reasons;
(f) if the pregnant woman, i.e. the married couple, has no separate dwelling.

Only about 1 per cent of the requests for induced abortions are refused.

Chapter 5

ATTITUDES TOWARDS FERTILITY DETERMINANTS AND THEIR INTERDEPENDENCE WITH FEMALE EMPLOYMENT

Alongside the increase in the economic activity of women in Hungary after the Second World War, fertility decreased. Given this trend, population policy must be based to a large extent on the attitude of working women. Measures to increase the number of births must take into account how women feel about their economic activity and professional careers. This question was examined by the Demographic Research Institute of the Hungarian Central Statistical Office in a survey carried out in 1978, "Opinions on family size and population policy" (Molnár and Pongrácz, 1980).[1] This survey focused on the factors affecting the willingness to give birth to children, among them the economic activity and professional career of the mother. The main purpose of the survey was to investigate both the material and the psychological factors exerting an influence on the willingness to give birth to children, especially to a third child. The research was based on interviews with relatively young mothers who already had two and three children and were therefore experienced in decisions on the birth of children.

1. Perceived Advantages and Disadvantages of More Children in Relation to Female Employment

Society has developed certain views as to the way and extent to which the birth of a child affects the life of the family. These opinions are connected with the parity of the future child because the birth of the first child influences the way of life and the functions of the family differently from the birth of the third child. There may be some factors which exert a positive effect on the life of the family at the birth of the first child but not at the birth of subsequent children. For example, the interpersonal relation between the parents could become closer through the birth of the first child. A similar impact might be felt even after the birth of the second child, but possibly much less than in the case of the first birth. Third and further children could even negatively affect the interpersonal relationships between the parents (the wife is overburdened, she is afraid of getting pregnant again, financial problems, etc.).

For these reasons, the study examined the perceived impact on family life of having children in one-, two- and three-child families. Mothers interviewed were asked to compare the well-being of families rearing one, two or three children, according to six aspects of family life. The respondents had to say whether, according to given aspects, the situation of one-child families was better, the same or worse than that of two-child families; and whether the situation of two-child families was better, the same or worse than that of three-child families. The comparison was based on the following factors:

(1)   Standard of living of the family
(2)   Economic activity of the mother
(3)   Development of the child's personality
(4)   Family atmosphere
(5)   The parents' relationship with each other
(6)   Esteem by the society

Though the purpose of this study was to analyse the interdependence between the mother's economic activity and the
willingness to give birth to children, a brief survey of the impact
of other factors was also undertaken, since the effect of the
mother's economic activity can be interpreted only in connection
with the other factors.

Of the six items indicated, two show a strong negative correlation with the willingness to increase the number of children: the
standard of living of the family and the mother's economic activity.
The majority of the respondents (around 70 per cent) thought that
having more children exerts a negative influence both on the
standard of living of the family and on the economic activity of the
mother.

According to the respondents, a clear positive correlation
exists between the development of the child's personality and the
number of children in the family in that it is generally accepted
that being a single child has a negative influence on the development of the child's personality.   Therefore the respondents
thought that the birth of a brother or sister would be definitely
favourable in this respect.   However, in the case of the second
brother/sister, the opinions were no longer unanimous.

As to the last three aspects investigated, neither a decisive
positive nor a decisive negative correlation can be stated.

With respect to the correlation between the mother's economic
activity and the number of children, there is a general view that a
higher number of children affects the mother's economic activity
negatively.   Behind this general statement, however, there are
different views according to demographic criteria.   Population
groups of different age and educational level attach different
importance to this aspect depending on the importance of economic
activity in the lives of the women.   Thus, young urban females
feel this impact more than women of older age groups or rural
females.   This factor plays a very great role among females with
a higher educational level and non-manual occupation who, in
general, do not work just to make money but consider their work
as a profession.   The significance of this question is well illus-
trated by the case of mothers of two children who are considering
whether to give birth to a third child.   As a reason for not
having a third child, females with a manual occupation put the
mother's employment in last place among the eight possible replies
(finding health, financial and housing problems, problems
connected with children's institutions and even the uncertainty of
the child's sex more important).   However, female professionals
put employment in second place after health problems.   Thus,
female professionals are of the opinion that three children would
hinder their work.   Feeling their work important, they decide in

advance not to give birth to a third child.

The female professionals' fear that more children may hinder their professional career is partly justified. Education statistics indicate that girls' chances for study and for continued education are the same as those for boys, and girls make use of this opportunity. In 1980, 65 per cent of the pupils in secondary schools were girls. In tertiary level education their proportion was almost equal to that of the boys and at some universities (faculties for teachers, economic and medical faculties) was even more than 50 per cent. However, after graduation, the professional career of females is handicapped. Female professionals finish their studies at the university or college at the age of 22-24 years, then take a job. In general they also marry at that age. Marriage in itself does not hinder women's economic activity. However, Hungarian fertility data indicate that, in the majority of young couples, children are born within the first few years of marriage. This means that, in the life of women, problems relating to the start of their career, to marriage and to childbirth arise at the same time. Under the impact of these three simultaneous events, the majority of young mothers are overburdened and are hindered in their working place, both professionally and financially.

Among economically active women, those with young children are in the most critical situation. Family help, which the former generation still received from the grandparents, can no longer be counted on because some of the grandparents are still economically active and can therefore give only limited child-care help. Thus, if the economic activity of females is required, the society has to take over part of the work of the family. This state and social assistance is given through the child-care allowance, crèches, kindergartens and the services facilitating household work.

2. Opinions on the Child-care Allowance

Information on, and a statistical analysis of, the child-care allowance are given in Chapter 2. Therefore, only the attitudes towards, and opinions on, the child-care allowance are discussed here.

The survey sample consisted of mothers with two or three children who, having married in 1966, gave birth to their children in or after 1967, i.e. after the introduction of the child-care allowance. Thus, their opinion on the advantages and disadvantages of the system is based on experience.

In studying the duration of the use of child-care leave, it emerged that though the overwhelming majority made use of this opportunity, only a few of them did so for the whole period of three years (see Chapter 2). Mothers doing professional work in general remained at home with their children for a shorter period (mostly for one and a half years) but for professional reasons they did not want to be absent from their working place for a longer period.

The question arises as to why the mothers interrupted their child-care leave and did not make use of the opportunity for three years (see table 5.1). The majority of those interviewed mentioned financial difficulties, i.e. that, because of the child-care leave, the total income of the family decreased and they were forced to go back to work to eliminate the difference between this lower income and the higher costs of living connected with the birth of the child. A relatively small proportion interrupted the three-year leave earlier for reasons connected with their working place. There is a positive correlation between the frequency of mentioning reasons of working place and per capita income, and there are significant differences by occupational group. A very high proportion of female professionals interrupted their child-care leave for reasons related to their work/working place. Though the monotony of household work and the risk of intellectual isolation were mentioned in the last place, still one-quarter of female professionals said that the reason for having interrupted their child-care leave was that the role of housewife did not satisfy their ambitions.

Table 5.1: Reasons for not using the child-care allowance for the full 3-year period [a] (in percentages)

Reason	%
Financial difficulties	41.3
She had succeeded in placing her child	20.8
Because of her working place	16.7
A further child was born [b]	37.0
The household did not satisfy her	5.5
Other causes	2.6

a   Some respondents gave more than one reason.

b   The mother temporarily returns to maternity leave, i.e. for a period of 20 weeks she receives pregnancy-confinement benefit equivalent to her total salary, which is more than the child-care allowance. Thus, child-care allowance is stopped and usually restarted 20 weeks later.

Source: Molnár and Pongrácz (1980).

There is no doubt that the child-care allowance was one of the most important measures in Hungarian population policy. Its main significance is not the stimulation of a willingness to give birth to children but rather the psychological and emotional effects created both for the mother and her child. In the first years of a child's life it is most difficult for a young and inexperienced mother to combine the work related to child-care with expectations at her place of work. The child-care allowance releases her from this double burden and permits her to concentrate only on maternal tasks. When speaking, however, of this positive impact of the child-care allowance, its negative features should be mentioned too. According to public opinion, the child-care allowance to a great extent preserves the unequal division of labour within the family. For young persons marrying at present, as compared to former generations, doing housework jointly is much more natural. This division of labour within the family changes greatly after the birth of the first child and during the subsequent child-care leave. The only tasks of a mother becoming temporarily a home-maker will be housework, child(ren's) care and education. Furthermore, to compensate for the loss of income, the husband sometimes takes a secondary job for the afternoon, evening or weekend. Thus, the husbands of women going back to work after child-care leave do not want to help their wives with work at home, as it has not been necessary for them to do so for two, three or even six years. For mothers re-entering employment, the continuation of the division of labour within the family developed during child-care leave produces a considerable double burden, both physical and psychological. Thus, the child-care allowance hinders the equalisation of the division of labour within the family and the development of the symmetrical family model.

Some of the mothers interviewed proposed to modify the decree on child-care allowance so as to restrain the development of the above tendencies. The child-care allowance regulations do not permit the mother to undertake paid work at home or part-time employment. However, the mothers, who have already made use of the child-care allowance and therefore can be considered as experienced, think that after the child is aged one to one and a half years they have some free time which could be spent on economic activity. Part-time employment in addition to the child-care allowance could decrease the financial problems of the family and release the husbands from the necessity of undertaking weekend or evening work. In this way, a more equal division of work within the family might be maintained and the symmetrical family model might survive the years of child-care leave.

There were some suggestions during the interviews to modify the decree on the child-care allowance by making it a legal possibility for fathers to make use of this allowance, i.e. to stay at home instead of the mother. Those who made this proposal thought that it would be better to leave the family to decide which family member, the mother or the father, wanted or was able to remain at home for a longer period. Alternatively, there were suggestions that for a certain period (one to one and a half years) only the mother should make use of the child-care leave and that after that the father should be able to make use of it. Although, at present, fathers can make use of the child-care leave in principle, it is very difficult to put this into practice. For attitudinal and financial reasons, the number of fathers on child-care leave is very low (around 100). The husband's salary is usually higher, and this is a very strong factor when deciding who should stay at home. It is significant that the women making such suggestions would like the fathers to take upon themselves a greater part of the care of young children, but the survey data indicate a rather great resistance on the part of the fathers. As will be seen below, fathers still consider child-care as primarily a maternal task and their participation is mainly limited to ensuring the children's physical and mental development.

3. Opinions Related to Child-care Institutions

An important condition of the continued employment of females is the creation and permanent development of child-care institutions. With the introduction of child-care leave, the kindergartens and day-time homes of schools attended by childen aged over 3 years became especially important. The studies examining the efficiency of the population policy measures indicate that there is a significant positive correlation between the quantity and quality of the provision of child-care services and the willingness to give birth to children. Among the different social services (i.e. getting a dwelling, the child-care allowance, family allowance, part-time job, etc.), "admission to a crèche, kindergarten" comes in second place after dwellings. This aspect is more important for residents of the capital and for female professionals. The reasons for this are the overcrowded child-care facilities in the capital and the concern of female graduates for their career.

In Hungary, as in other socialist countries, the overwhelming majority of children spend some period of their life in child-care institutions, crèches, kindergartens and day-time homes at school. The present survey investigated whether economically active mothers consider this as a constraint or as a desirable arrangement, and whether mothers think it is better for a child to be educated at home, or in a community or an institution for children at various ages. The age groups were developed in conformity with the existing forms of child-care institutions, with the difference that the crèche age (0-3 year(s)) was divided into two stages: the period until the age of 1 year which is considered very important for the relationship between the mother and her child, and the following period of the age of 1-3 year(s).

It was the unanimous opinion of those interviewed that it is very important for children under 1 year of age to be cared for by the mother herself because the strong emotional relation developing between mother and child at that time is decisive for the child's physical and mental development. There were somewhat fewer mothers of the opinion that this is also best at the age of 1-3 year(s); however, they still represented the majority.

Education in a community first becomes important in the case of children aged 3-6 years. According to the general view, it is important and necessary that children of 3-6 years should attend a kindergarten and should be influenced not only by the family but also by the community. In the case of children attending primary school (aged 6-14 years), the preference for home education (i.e. after school hours) increases again. This is mainly related to the crowded nature of day-time school homes and to their poor quality.

Mothers feel that, after the age of 0-3 year(s), it is in the early years of school that both the mother and the child bear the greatest physical burden; and these difficulties could be eased either by better day-time school home provision or by shortening the mother's working time through a part-time job.

4. Use of Child-care Institutions

Some of the effects of the above-mentioned attitudes and opinions on family size were shown in the 1980 longitudinal surveys. The availability of child-care near the place of residence and its relation to the number of living children and the total number of children desired were investigated for the first time. Crèches and kindergartens were considered in particular because they directly affected the couples covered by the survey in the sixth year of marriage.

It should be mentioned that child-care leave is an institution which can replace a crèche. Some 85 per cent of the women covered by the sample said that there was a crèche in the neighbourhood of their residence but 70 per cent of them did not want to make use of it. This was due to the use of the child-care allowance or to the fact that they had no child under 3 years. Some 15 per cent of the two-child mothers, 6 per cent of the one-child mothers and 9 per cent of the three-child mothers made use of the crèches at the date of the survey. The proportion who could not make use of a crèche near their place of residence was only 2.8 per cent (see table 5.2). They were mainly dependent women who were not entitled to it, but also among agricultural manual workers this proportion was double the average. A total of 15 per cent of the women declared that there was no crèche near their residence. Among rural women, this share reached 31 per cent but in urban areas it was only 4.5 per cent. However, only somewhat more than one-half of females belonging to this group would make use of the crèche if there were such a service near their residence.

The situation is different with respect to kindergartens. The supply is better and they are used to a far greater extent than crèches. Only 4 per cent of the women indicated that there was no kindergarten near their residence. Two-thirds of the women questioned made use of the kindergarten at the date of the survey. Three-quarters of the women with two children belonged to this group; among the three- and four-child families, this proportion was below average.

In respect of kindergartens, a higher proportion of women declared that although there was a kindergarten near their residence, they were not able to make use of it. Some 6-7 per cent of two-child mothers and 9 per cent of three-child mothers belonged to this group. Here, too, the female's economic activity played an important role but also the share of females belonging to this group was higher among manual workers than among non-manual workers.

Due to fertility differences by region and occupation, women with the most children were in the majority among those who

Table 5.2: Supply and use of crèches and kindergartens by number of living children and residence (in percentages)

No. of living children 1980	Children's institution exists near residence			No children's institution near residence		Total
	They make use of it	They cannot make use of it	They do not need it	They would make use of it	They would not make use of it	
	Crèche					
1	6.5	1.4	80.2	5.4	6.5	100.0
2	15.5	3.9	61.5	11.3	7.8	100.0
3	10.0	4.9	60.1	14.9	10.1	100.0
4	8.2	3.3	70.5	4.9	13.1	100.0
Total	10.8	2.8	70.6	8.5	7.3	100.0
	Kindergarten					
1	69.4	2.4	25.8	2.3	0.3	100.0
2	73.5	6.6	14.2	5.4	0.3	100.0
3	65.5	8.9	20.8	4.8	0.0	100.0
4	58.1	8.1	27.3	6.5	0.0	100.0
Total	66.2	4.7	24.8	3.9	0.4	100.0

Residence			Crèche			
Budapest	16.1	2.6	74.8	3.8	2.7	100.0
Other urban areas	14.0	2.5	79.0	2.6	1.9	100.0
Rural areas	5.3	3.0	60.9	16.3	14.4	100.0
Total	10.7	2.8	70.7	8.5	7.3	100.0
			Kindergarten			
Budapest	60.3	2.8	31.2	4.5	1.2	100.0
Other urban areas	67.2	3.8	26.3	2.5	0.2	100.0
Rural areas	67.8	6.4	20.6	4.9	0.3	100.0
Total	66.2	4.7	24.8	3.9	0.4	100.0

Source: Provisional results not yet published of the 1980 follow-up survey of persons married in 1974.

mentioned lack of supply or their failure to use such institutions. Among them, the share of one-child families was far below average and the proportion of three-child families was about twice as high. Thus, the females reporting a lack of institutional care had so far given birth to the most children and also the total number of their planned children was the highest.

Another aspect of child-care can be studied if the type of care by age of child is examined. The changing role and significance of children's institutions and the family can be seen according to the age of children. This process was studied for all first children. According to the results, in more than 90 per cent of the cases in which the child was less than 1 year of age, the mother was at home. Among them, the proportion of mothers having made use of the child-care allowance was 83 per cent. Only 3-4 per cent of the mothers indicated the crèche as a form of care for children under the age of 1 year. The proportion of mothers who charged the grandparents with the rearing of their child under the age of 1 year was somewhat higher. Though decreasing by child's age, until the child's age is 3 years, mothers mostly remained at home to care for their children. Between the ages of 1 and 2 years nearly 80 per cent of the mothers, and between the ages of 2 and 3 years about 70 per cent cared for their children at home.

With the increase in the children's age, the role of crèches and grandparents in day-time care grows. At the age of 1-2 years about 12 per cent, and at the age of 2-3 years more than 20 per cent of the children were placed in crèches. The grandparents care for 5-7 per cent of the children at these ages.

Over the age of 3 years, the kindergarten takes over the principal role in day-time care. Nearly 80 per cent of the mothers indicated the kindergarten as the form of their children's care at the age of 3-6 years. Besides, more than 10 per cent of the mothers were also at home at this age, making use of child-care leave not with the first but with the second or third child. The grandparents' role in children's care at the age of 3-6 years decreased to less than 3 per cent.

At the date of the survey, relatively few women (8 per cent) had children of school age. According to the data, at school age there was no main form of child-care similar to child-care leave for children under 3 years or to kindergarten at the age of 3-6 years. At the beginning of school age, the majority of children (55 per cent) were placed in the day-time homes of primary schools, about 20 per cent of the mothers were at home either because they were on child-care leave with younger children or because they were dependent. With the increase in school age, the role of the day-time homes of schools decreases and that of the grandparents gets continuously more important in the child's care. The proportion of children staying at home alone after school grows according to age. This share was 8 per cent for the pupils of the third and fourth year classes (at the age of 8-9 years) and 20 per cent for the fifth class (over the age of 10 years).

Table 5.3: Characteristic types of care for first child at various ages (in percentages)

Age of children	Way of care for children								
	The mother is		Crèche	Kinder-garten	Day-time home of primary school[b]	The child is alone at home	Grand-parents	Other	Total
	depend-ent	on child-care leave[a]							
Until the age of 1 year	8.0	83.7	3.1	-	-	-	3.4	1.8	100.0
At the age of 1-2 years	6.5	73.8	12.1	0.0	-	-	5.4	2.2	100.0
At the age of 2-3 years	5.7	62.8	21.0	0.9	-	-	7.2	2.4	100.0
At the age of 3-6 years	3.8	11.6	-	80.4	0.0	0.0	2.8	1.4	100.0
Primary school:									
Class 1-2 years	10.5	9.7	-	1.1	55.7	2.8	13.0	7.2	100.0
Class 3-4 years	6.1	7.6	-	0.4	51.3	7.6	16.4	10.6	100.0
Class 5 years	5.9	5.9	-	-	35.8	20.8	18.2	13.4	100.0

a For children over 3 years the mother is at home on child-care leave with another child under 3 years.

b In spite of the limited number of school children observed in the survey, the proportion attending day-time homes in primary school is similar to those indicated in current education statistics for school year 1982-83: class 1-2, 66.0; class 3-4, 55.1; class 5, 30.9.

Source: Provisional data not yet published of the 1980 follow-up survey of persons married in 1974.

5.   Housing Conditions and Fertility

In the 1978 survey carried out by the Demographic Research Institute of the Hungarian Central Statistical Office, "getting a dwelling" came in first place among those social services which affected the willingness to give birth to children.   Therefore, the results on the interdependence of fertility and housing conditions from the longitudinal marriage surveys are given here.

Naturally, most young couples would prefer to begin their common life in a separate dwelling.   But only about 20 per cent of the young couples under 35 years married in 1966 had a separate dwelling at marriage.   This means that four-fifths of the couples married without a final solution to their housing conditions. Among them, those couples who could live temporarily in the dwelling of their parents, relatives or acquaintances were in the best position to finance a separate dwelling;   two-thirds of the couples started their common life in such a way.   More than 10 per cent, however, lived in subtenancies;   in respect of housing, they were in the worst situation.[2]

Eight years later, among couples married in 1974, the proportion of those having a separate dwelling at marriage remained the same.   The proportion, however, who lived as family members with their parents or relatives decreased;   the ratio of those living in subtenancies and temporarily separately from one another grew.

It is difficult to state a uniform relation between plans concerning family size and housing conditions at marriage.   Most marrying couples consider their housing conditions at marriage only as a temporary solution;   however, they envisage their family plans for a longer period, even if later they are forced to modify these plans.   Nevertheless, couples living in their own separate dwelling plan a somewhat greater family size.

A uniform and rapid improvement in housing conditions can be observed in the first years of marriage.   Six years after marriage, the housing conditions of 70 per cent of the women married in 1966 were solved.   The number of owners of dwellings grew by 500 per cent and that of subtenants fell by one-third. The share of couples living as family members with others - who represented two-thirds of the total number of marrying couples at marriage - was only 25 per cent 6 years later.   The proportion of couples living as tenants increased to a small extent and the proportion of couples living in service dwellings was somewhat more than 6 per cent.

Among the couples married in 1974, the situation was less favourable.   Fewer couples began their married life in the dwellings of their parents and more as subtenants.   More than one-half of the couples were owners of dwellings five and a half years after marriage and, together with those living as tenants or in service dwellings, three-quarters lived in separate dwellings. The relatively high proportion starting married life in sub-tenancies, however, fell greatly and in 1980 fewer couples lived in subtenancies than did those who married in 1966, after a similar duration of marriage.   It was also true, however, that the proportion of couples living as tenants and in service dwellings was

Table 5.4: Tenure of dwelling at marriage (1974) and in the sixth year of marriage (1980) by wife's socio-occupational group and residence (in percentages)

	Tenure							Total
	Owners	Family members of owners	Tenants	Family members of tenants	Sub-tenants	Service dwelling tenants	Other	
Occupation								
Economically active of which:								
Non-agricultural manual workers 1974	12.4	54.3	4.0	11.7	13.0	0.5	4.1	100.0
1980	51.1	22.4	13.1	3.7	5.0	4.1	0.7	100.0
Agricultural manual workers 1974	18.3	63.4	4.9	3.5	5.9	2.5	1.5	100.0
1980	61.6	23.3	3.8	1.3	1.9	7.5	0.6	100.0
Non-manual workers 1974	13.4	41.6	6.1	15.7	15.0	1.0	7.2	100.0
1980	50.5	16.3	17.6	6.3	2.7	5.7	0.9	100.0
Dependants 1974	13.3	50.6	4.2	12.9	9.7	0.9	8.4	100.0
1980	60.0	21.7	6.2	3.4	2.8	4.8	1.0	100.0
Total 1974	13.1	49.3	4.9	13.2	13.2	0.8	5.6	100.0
1980	51.7	19.7	14.4	4.7	3.8	5.0	0.8	100.0
Residence								
Budapest 1974	10.2	21.7	7.5	35.6	10.8	0.4	13.8	100.0
1980	27.0	13.0	32.2	17.8	3.8	3.5	2.7	100.0
Other urban areas 1974	11.8	46.3	5.9	13.3	17.8	0.8	4.1	100.0
1980	53.9	14.7	17.3	3.2	4.7	5.4	0.8	100.0
Rural areas 1974	14.8	59.9	3.4	5.6	11.4	1.0	3.9	100.0
1980	59.9	27.0	3.9	0.7	2.8	5.1	0.2	100.0
Total 1974	13.1	49.3	4.9	13.1	13.2	0.8	5.6	100.0
1980	51.7	19.7	14.4	4.7	3.8	5.0	0.8	100.0

Sources: 1. Hungarian Central Statistical Office (1979b).
2. The 1980 data are the results of the provisional processing not yet published.

lower than among the couples married eight years earlier.

Regional differences in housing conditions at marriage (1974) changed somewhat by 1980. As was true of the situation five and a half years earlier, the proportion of couples having a separate dwelling was still the lowest in the capital (though it also grew by 350 per cent) and the proportion living with parents declined the least.

The housing conditions of couples in provincial towns were the most favourable; more than three-quarters of them lived in their own, separate dwelling. However, similarly to the situation at marriage, the proportion of couples living in subtenancies five and a half years later was also the highest.

The housing conditions of couples exert a great impact on the size of the family they actually have (table 5.5). At the beginning of married life, there were not yet great differences in ideas on family size according to housing conditions. In the actual number of children three or six years later, however, there were great differences according to housing conditions. This is confirmed by the results of both longitudinal surveys after a similar duration of marriage. It can be stated that, after a marriage duration of both three and six years, the average number of children in families living in a separate dwelling was higher than in those living with parents as family members or in subtenancies. The results also indicate that the improvement in the housing conditions over the last 15 years exerted a positive impact on attitudes to fertility. Among the couples married in 1974, not only was the proportion of those living in a separate dwelling higher but also their average number of children was higher than for the marriage cohort married eight years earlier under similar conditions. It should be mentioned that in 1980 the existence or lack of a separate dwelling was related to the average number of children to a far greater extent than eight years earlier when the marriage duration of the couples married in 1966 was similar.

Having or not having a separate dwelling influenced not only the number of children already born but also the total number planned, although to a lesser extent. Not only was the number of children born to couples living in their parents' dwelling the smallest, but their planned completed family size was also somewhat lower.

The improvement in the housing conditions can also be shown on the basis of the change in the number of rooms. In 1966, three-quarters of the couples under age 35 years began their common life in one room, 13 per cent in two rooms and only 3 per cent in three or more rooms. In the least favourable situation were those who had no separate room (5 per cent), and those couples living separately after their marriage (4-5 per cent). The lack of a separate room and living separately temporarily were most frequent in the capital (about 20 per cent). In 1980, about 50 per cent of the couples married in 1974 lived in two rooms, more than one-third of them in three or more rooms. The proportion of one-room dwellings (occupied by three-quarters of the couples immediately after marriage) fell to 17 per cent. In the capital the share of couples living in one-room dwellings was the

Table 5.5: Plans concerning family size and average number of living children by housing tenure

Number of children	Tenure							Total
	Owners	Family members of owners	Tenants	Family members of tenants	Sub-tenants	Service dwelling	Other	
	Average number of children							
Planned at marriage (1974)	2.20	2.17	2.22	2.18	2.18	2.14	2.18	2.17
Living (1980)	1.65	1.46	1.63	1.26	1.44	1.55	1.47	1.58
Planned at present[a] (1980)	1.99	1.90	1.98	1.73	1.94	1.98	2.00	1.97

a Sum of the average number of living children and children desired additionally.

Source: See table 5.4.

highest and in the provincial towns the lowest. Among rural families, the proportion living in three or more rooms was already as high as the proportion of those who lived in two-room dwellings (42 per cent each).

The proportion of dependent women living in one room was much higher and that of persons living in three or more rooms was lower than among economically active females. Of economically active women, non-manual workers were in the most favourable situation, and the housing conditions of the agricultural manual workers were the least favourable.

The relationship between the number of children and the number of rooms is not quite uniform due to differences by residence and occupation. Table 5.6 shows that for women living in Budapest, the number of actual and planned children tends to increase with a third and fourth room in the dwelling (more so for the number planned). However, for women outside Budapest, there is no strong relationship between the size of the dwelling and their actual or desired family size. Nevertheless, for rural women there is a slight tendency for larger dwellings to be related to smaller numbers of actual and desired children.

Table 5.6: Average number of living and desired children of females married in 1974 by the number of rooms and residence of the women six years after marriage, 1980

Residence	Number of rooms					Total
	No separate room[a]	1	2	3	4-9	
Living children						
Budapest	0.88	1.44	1.41	1.67	1.90	1.51
Other towns	1.17	1.58	1.59	1.70	1.52	1.61
Villages	1.67	1.71	1.69	1.63	1.56	1.66
Total	1.20	1.60	1.60	1.66	1.60	1.62
Desired children						
Budapest	1.50	1.98	1.88	2.99	2.25	1.95
Other towns	2.17	2.03	1.99	2.05	1.94	2.01
Villages	2.00	2.11	2.04	2.03	1.96	2.04
Total	1.85	2.05	1.99	2.03	2.00	2.01

[a] Number of cases is 20.

Source: See table 5.4, source 2.

In the sixth year of marriage, about one-half of the couples mentioned that they intended to change their housing conditions. Nearly two-thirds of the couples living in the capital belonged to this group, and their number was the lowest in the provincial towns. Of the couples desiring to change their housing conditions, the majority (29 per cent) wanted to do so through allocation by the local council. The proportion of those intending to improve their housing conditions through an exchange of dwelling or by increasing the size of the dwelling was the same. More than 20 per cent of those desiring to move to another dwelling wanted to build a family house; however, 6-7 per cent of them wanted to buy a co-operative dwelling. Women who had considered their housing conditions as final in the sixth year of marriage gave birth to somewhat more children than those who intended to change their housing conditions. Among the latter, however, those desiring to have a family house and those intending to increase the size of their existing dwelling had the most children.

It can also be remarked that families wanting to change their present housing conditions desired slightly more children than those which had no intention to do so (table 5.7). It was a question of the timing of childbirths, i.e. waiting for better housing conditions, because families desiring to move into another dwelling had fewer living children than those not intending to change. The largest families were planned by couples intending to move into a new dwelling through construction of a family house.

Table 5.7: Average number of living and desired children
of females married in 1974, 1980

	Average number of children	
	Living	Desired
Intends to change dwellings	1.58	2.03
by constructing a family house	1.62	2.08
by getting a flat	1.57	1.98
Does not intend to change dwellings	1.65	1.99

Source: See table 5.4, source 2.

6. Household Work of Economically Active Females

The influence of household work on female employment is important. The conflicts resulting from the co-ordination of household work and tasks at work could be decreased by the partial socialisation of family work (through services) on the one hand and by increased mechanisation of housework on the other hand. This is especially important in that, according to the results of the time budget studies (see Chapter 4), contrary to expectation, the duration of household work has not shortened very much.

Mechanisation of housework, use of services and even the division of family labour depend on the financial situation of the family. In families with a number of children and a low income, current expenditure impedes the mechanisation of housework. The majority of families who require household services and who are able to pay for them are of a high educational level, and therefore have a relatively high income. The services the families use most frequently are canteen meals which replace time-intensive buying, cooking and washing up. Thus, the use of services is mainly characteristic of the groups with better financial conditions and of the groups in which the wife does professional work requiring a high qualification.

Under the impact of several factors (e.g. social and environmental factors, the change in the quality of needs, their differentiation), housework has become lighter. However, its duration has not decreased and presumably will not decrease in the future either. The traditional division of family labour is still generally characteristic of present Hungarian society. Housework is done mainly by the wife and this prolongs the disadvantageous situation of women within the society and the family as compared to men. According to the data of the time budget survey, the total working time (household work included) of economically active females is longer than that of economically active males. Married men spend on average 84 minutes per day on housework and 25 minutes on looking after the children, compared to married women who spend 260 minutes and 32 minutes, respectively, in these activities. In general for women with manual occupations, the "second shift" lasts about four hours per day and, for females with non-manual occupations, it lasts on average less than three hours daily. Thus, social stratification produces a longer daily working time for the lower occupational groups of economically active females. The proportion of women engaged mostly in housework is, naturally, the highest among the inactive earners, i.e. home-makers, pensioners and mothers on child-care leave. The average daily working time of the latter is more than five hours, plus they spend two or two and a half hours daily on child-care. Thus, it can be stated that care for the family as a unit is still a typically female task and that husbands participate less in household work and concentrate most of their assistance on child education.

7. Views on the Division of Labour by Sex Within the Family and Female Employment

The public opinion survey of the Demographic Research Institute of the Hungarian Central Statistical Office concerning population policy also examined the views of women and men with children on the question of employment in order to determine how female employment could be moderated so as to eliminate conflicts resulting from female work in the family and at work. Males and females were asked whether a mother with a child under 14 years should continue her economic activity or whether she should interrupt it or even give it up and live only to fulfil her family work. The replies reflected approval of the traditional division of labour. According to the majority (66 per cent), a mother with child(ren) should remain at home because the child(ren)'s education, housekeeping and the creation of a favourable family atmosphere are the most important tasks for her. The minority who approved of a woman with a child continuing her economic activity, indicated first of all financial reasons, and mentioned only in second place that a woman could not be satisfied by household work alone. There were, however, rather great differences in views by sex, residence and occupational groups. A greater proportion of males (70 per cent against 63 per cent of females) was of the opinion that the traditional social division of female labour should be maintained. The opinion that a woman could not be satisfied by household work alone was maintained more frequently by professional females (64 per cent).

With regard to differences of view according to area of settlement, the proportion who considered the woman's household functions as the most important was the lowest in Budapest and the highest in rural areas. Rural residents gave the tasks related to the child's education as the reason for this. Those considering it necessary for mothers with young children to maintain their economic activity gave financial reasons (i.e. the woman's earning capacity was also needed) in an equal proportion by settlement categories, while female emancipation was emphasised in Budapest more frequently than in rural areas. The residents of provincial towns were in the middle between Budapest and the rural areas in respect of all opinions.

There was a strong correlation between the occupational group of those interviewed and the views for or against the continuation of the economic activity of a woman with children. In general those with manual occupations (as well as dependants and inactive earners) considered more frequently than those with non-manual occupations that a mother should give up her occupation or interrupt it temporarily and should live only for her family and children. However, in the opinion of the majority of female professionals, a woman could not be satisfied by housekeeping alone; they deemed it necessary to ensure that care for their children was provided in a form (mainly in institutions for children) which did not impede the mother from pursuing her profession.

In the study of the factors affecting the willingness to give birth to children, the views of mothers with two and more children were asked concerning the conflicts and problems of co-ordination of their tasks at home and at work. Three possible solutions were mentioned and they were asked to choose the one which they found the best:

1. If the husband's income were sufficient to support the family while the wife looked after the family and dealt with house-keeping,

2. If the wife worked for a shorter time to have more time for the family and household,

3. If both the husband and wife worked and divided the child's education and the household work in equal proportion.

On average, 37 per cent of the mothers found it best if the husband were able to support the family from his income and the wife looked after the family.

The next alternative in the questionnaire (chosen by 35 per cent) mentioned the possibility of the wife's working shorter hours so as to have more time for the family and household work. This alternative did not exclude the woman's employment outside home, but again burdened the woman with family and household work, i.e. she should work for a shorter time so that she can be a better mother and housewife. Therefore, the proportion (24 per cent) who considered as desirable the way of life in which the partners (husband and wife) are economically active and divide the household work in an equal proportion was rather low. Interestingly, not only the older generation favoured the traditional division of labour in the family; 47 per cent of mothers under 30 years with three children said that only the husband should be economically active and that the income should be sufficient to support the whole family.

By settlement areas, the view that the woman should remain at home was most frequent in rural areas and it was much less frequent in Budapest. Mainly the residents of Budapest and other urban areas considered the part-time work of females as ideal for the co-ordination of family and work. The division of labour in the family based on bearing equal burdens (both partners economically active and dividing household work in an equal proportion) seemed to be most popular among females with three children living in Budapest and least popular among rural females with three children.

The distribution of views by socio-economic group indicates that the division of household and family tasks in an equal proportion was mostly accepted by female professionals. These women denied that females should do only household work, and the majority of them considered shorter working time as the best solution. Besides the professionals, women of other non-manual occupations also supported the idea of part-time jobs for mothers with children. The view that the household and the family are enough for a mother was most popular among dependants and manual workers.

Thus, the views indicate that, because of the difficulties in co-ordinating their double burden, women would like to change this situation. As they do not want to give up the oldest female function, motherhood, some of them consider that the solution lies in renouncing their occupation or profession. Others think that the economic activity of women is the reason for problems with the child's education and for the difficulties in family life. It is obvious, however, that the majority of economically active women cannot leave their employment just to fulfil better their role as a mother and housewife. Most women, whether they are aware of it or not, need some employment, or profession, in their own interest. This is also confirmed by women's view on child-care leave who feel that in addition to their professional handicap, their situation within the family is also affected negatively by the three (or often two times three) years spent on child-care leave.

Female employment is necessary for the family's economic well-being as well. At present, the majority of families would be unable to meet the increasing financial demands from one salary. At the same time, society requires the work of females. Under the present labour conditions, the economy cannot do without the female labour force, which represents 43.9 per cent of the economically active population.

Recently, there has been an increasing demand among women for part-time work or reduced working hours. While the government supports the idea, some employers are reluctant and/or limited by technical factors.

Therefore, the question arises as to what society can do in the long term to lessen the tensions and work deriving from the double burden of women who have to combine their household tasks with those at work. These surveys show that according to the female respondents, one of the main policies society could adopt would be to take over family work, to a greater extent than at present, by developing qualitatively and quantitatively the network of child-care institutions and widening the range of services available. At present, the insufficent quantity, and often quality, of services causes problems.

The subjective precondition of any further change is to alter attitudes so that the democratic system of the division of labour within the family becomes more general and more acceptable than it is at present. The problems of the combination of work and maternal duties are related to the scope of tasks of the father in the family and to the combination of his work and paternal duties. The equal chance of females to participate in socially organised work can be realised only if the burdens in the family are borne equally.

Notes

1   The sample survey covered 1,867 males (between 18-60 years) and 1,970 females (between 18-55 years). The frame of the sample was the total population (1970 census) in these age groups.

2   The subtenant rents a room or a part of the dwelling from the tenant/owner. Although subtenancy may be suitable for single students, bachelors, etc., it is generally disadvantageous for a couple because: (a) the rent of subtenancy is higher, being the free market price; and (b) kitchen, bathroom, etc., usually have to be shared with the tenant/ owner. The service dwelling is given by the employer; it is usually restricted to the period of employment.

Appendix

DESCRIPTION OF THE METHODOLOGY OF LONGITUDINAL MARRIAGE SURVEYS

Definition of Concepts

Family planning means the plan and attitude of married couples and couples not married but living together with reference to the decision on the desired number of children as well as on the timing of childbirths. Some spouses already have a definite view on the size of their family at the date of marriage, whereas others develop the family planning ideas later, e.g. after the birth of the first or more children. Those women who determined the desired number of children at the time of marriage were considered as family planners prior to marriage. In the follow-up surveys, those women who could definitely state how many children they desired in addition to their living children were considered as family planners.

1. Educational level

Study completed successfully at day or evening schools or correspondence courses run by organised school education. Here the educational level is indicated by the total number of years completed at primary, secondary and tertiary level schools. The number of years completed at apprentice schools is not included.

2. Socio-occupational groups

For the socio-occupational grouping, the occupations both of the woman and her husband were taken into consideration. If a woman had an occupation (i.e. was economically active) she was included in the respective socio-occupational group by her own occupation; if she had no occupation (i.e. dependent) then her husband's occupation was used.
Three major groups were distinguished:
- agricultural manual workers;
- non-agricultural manual workers;
- non-manual workers.

3. Planned number of children/desired number of children

In this material, the "planned number of children" means the number of children planned at marriage.
Therefore, only those women who already had an idea of the number of their future children before marriage can have "planned children". The plans developed during marriage and the changes in the original plans are considered under "desired number of children".

4. Number of additional children desired/total number of children desired

The "number of additional children desired" is the number of children desired in addition to the living children. The "total number of children desired" is the sum of the number of children living at the dates of the surveys and the number of additional children desired.

Description of the Methodology of Longitudinal Marriage Surveys

The preparation, planning and execution of family planning, fertility and birth control surveys raise a number of special methodological questions. As they are relevant to the results and their evaluation, it is necessary to describe them briefly.

1. Selection of the sample and its characteristics

Because of special difficulties in connection with selection and organisation, the majority of family planning studies cannot represent the whole country. Most questions are considered as delicate "intimate" issues and, therefore, in the past, the majority of data collections of this kind investigated only the limited area of some health institutions or towns.

The main purpose of the longitudinal marriage surveys started in 1966 and 1974 was to select a sample suitable not only for making statements and drawing conclusions for the entire country but also for allowing the evaluation of data by the three main settlement areas: the capital, other urban areas and rural areas. Besides, the sample had to represent the three major occupational groups: agricultural manual workers, non-agricultural manual workers and non-manual workers.

When determining the proportion and the size of the sample, the follow-up of the selected couples (with several repeated interviews) for 10-15 years, during which time many drop-outs would be unavoidable, had to be taken into consideration. At the same time, the sample size was also limited by the financial means available and by the capacity for carrying out the survey. On this basis, the selection of a 5 per cent sample seemed expedient. This implied the selection of about 4,700 engaged couples marrying in 1966 and about 5,000 engaged couples marrying in 1974.

For the 1966 sample, a two-stage selection procedure was used. The primary sampling unit was the settlement (villages and towns), and the secondary sampling unit was the couples desiring to marry. The vital registration statistics on marriages contracted in Hungary in 1964 served as a framework for sampling. A stratified sample was selected in villages and provincial towns. For the villages, 49 categories were developed on the basis of population and the number of marriages. Besides considering the given sampling fraction by counties and categories, enough sample villages had to be selected through a systematic selection method of equal probability to ensure that the number of marriages contracted there would be equal to at least 5 per cent of the yearly total number of marriages contracted in rural areas. For this minimum, 6-7 per cent of the villages of the country had to be included in the sample in such a way that in villages with a population under 2,000 all engaged couples were included in the sample. Actually, 8 per cent of the villages of the country (258 villages) were included in the 1966 sample. This represented 5.4 per cent of marriages contracted in villages.

For the towns, two categories by population size, numbering over 40,000 and under 40,000 respectively, were developed. Then, the population of the towns under 40,000 was further broken down by occupational structure, i.e. industrial, agricultural and mixed categories. From the four strata thus developed, every second town was included in the sample by systematic selection. Budapest and all the towns of county status were automatically included in the sample. Altogether, 31 towns (53 per cent of the towns) were selected in 1966.

A selection list kept by chronological order in the rural and urban registration districts served as a basis for the selection of secondary sample units. The couples were selected from the list by the registrars on the basis of the sampling fraction given by settlements and applying a random starting number. Altogether, 5.2 per cent of the marriages contracted in 1966 (4,622 married couples) were included.

The 1974 selection was based on the settlement list of the 1966 sample. However, this time it was not deemed expedient to select the couples during a whole year as had been done in 1966. The selection of the couples to be included in the sample was reduced to half a year in such a way that in a great number of the given settlements the sampling fraction was doubled. The number of small villages, where the sampling fraction of marrying couples was 100 per cent in 1966, however, also had to be doubled. In 1974, 405 villages (13 per cent of Hungarian villages) were included in the sample. As the number of towns in the country had grown in the meantime, 39 towns (51 per cent of the towns) were included in the sample in 1974. Budapest and the towns of county status were selected in 1974, too.

The secondary sampling units (the marrying couples) were selected, as for 1966, on the basis of the selection list kept by chronological order. Altogether, 11 per cent of marriages contracted in the second half of 1974 (5,257 couples) were included in the sample which was equal to 5.7 per cent of the total number of marriages in 1974.

The distribution of our sample data was compared by some main criteria with data for the whole country. For this, we calculated the confidence limits of certain relative frequencies at a 95 per cent confidence level. The results showed that in the distribution by the main criteria (e.g. by age group, socio-occupational group and educational level) the overwhelming majority of the national data were within the confidence limits calculated by the sample data. Thus, it could be safely assumed that sample distributions by other criteria, depending on the above factors, corresponded well to the national data.

It is characteristic of the sample data of both surveys that the proportion of the younger age group and of persons of a higher educational level was somewhat higher, while the share of agricultural, manual workers and of dependants was somewhat lower, than in the national data.

Overall, the samples were adequate to furnish data on the subjects investigated. They indicated the differences between females (and couples) of different residence, social level, educational level, etc.

2. Subjects, organisations and follow-up

Some of the subjects in the family planning studies refer to intimate aspects of human life; therefore, the selection of appropriate interviewers is crucial. Health visitors working in the field of mother and infant care are trusted by the people and have the qualifications and experience for data collection on such delicate subjects. Therefore, in agreement with the Ministry of Health, the health visitors were invited to take part in the data collection.

In 1966 the registrars selected the sample of marrying persons and carried out the interviewing. The majority of the questions concerned basic demographic information, housing conditions, the circumstances of getting acquainted and the family planning ideas of the couples.

After the 1966 basic survey, all the follow-up interviews were carried out by health visitors. Follow-up interviews were performed in 1969, 1972, 1975 and 1980.

The sample of couples marrying in 1974 was selected at the premarriage medical consultation introduced the same year. Participation in the consultation is compulsory for all couples under 35 years intending to marry. Thus, only couples under 35 years were included in the 1974 sample.

After the 1974 basic survey, the health visitors again visited the couples covered by the sample in their homes in 1977 and 1980. Also, on this occasion, the questions were directed only towards wives. The main questions were plans concerning family size, fertility history and birth control practice. Of the influencing factors, the housing situation, income and occupation were always covered. During the individual surveys additional information was collected on some topical subjects. Such questions were: the reasons for, and circumstances of, abortion; views and suggestions on the 1973 population policy measures; the reasons for the use or non-use of the child-care allowance.

A new phase in the longitudinal follow-up marriage surveys took place at the end of 1980. The females married in 1966 were interviewed at home for the fifth time and those married in 1974 for the third time by the health visitors conducting the survey.

The 1980 survey also represented part of the international study organised by the International Labour Office with the purpose of stating the relationship between female's role in socio-economic life and the development of their fertility. The subjects relevant to this issue were: the division of labour within the family; family life; the daily timetable; occupational history; care for and rearing of children.

The analysis is mainly based on the data of the 1980 survey processed by some main criteria. First the data of the 1974 marriage cohort were processed, as the fertility situation of the present and the near future is primarily determined by the fertility attitude of women under 30 years and by the factors affecting this attitude. At the end of 1980, 87 per cent of the females covered by the sample of the 1974 marriage cohort were under 30 years. Thus, our data characterise not only a marriage cohort but to some extent the total married female population under 30 years of age.

The data of 4,717 respondent females were processed. This number represents 91 per cent of the initial 1974 sample. Only 6 per cent of the women included in the sample were dependent; about 30 per cent of the economically active females were on child-care leave at the date of the survey. The distribution of the sample data by residence and educational level as well as the composition of economically active women by occupation character-ised the differences by regions, educational level and occupations.

3. Checking, correction and processing of data

After each survey, the data were corrected both manually and by computer. The first screening of data began simultaneously with the enumeration. This is very important because at the start of the survey systematic errors of the enumerators as well as errors resulting from misunderstandings can still be eliminated. This checking and correcting operation was carried out by the leading health visitors of the counties, towns, and districts, charged with the direction and organisation of the local work, in co-operation with the central instructors.

At the end of the enumeration, questionnaires were sent for central revision. Besides controlling their completeness, the editors had to correct the errors and inconsistent answers as indicated in the instruction for revision. The questionnaire of the earlier survey was also considered during the revision. The editors' additional task was to classify the replies given in the so-called open-ended questions.

The revised questionnaires were coded. The basic document for this work was the coding manual which already contained the elements necessary for checking and correcting by computer. The data were then fixed on magnetic tapes.

In the case of longitudinal studies, there are different possi-bilities for data processing. One of them is to process the data of the individual according to the same aspects, separately, directly after the individual enumerations. This method of pro-cessing furnishes data comparable also in time on certain subjects. In this case, however, it should be taken into consideration that, due to the drop-outs, the results concerning the different dates (different duration of marriage) refer to a different number of women interviewed.

The other method of processing is to fix on one record all data collected at different dates on the same women. In the case of women married in 1966, this means that the life of a woman can be followed from the date of marriage until the 1980 enumeration, i.e. until the fifteenth year of marriage, on the same record. This method of processing is more difficult technically and it raises a number of methodological problems but the results are more exact. In such cases the results concern only a part of the females included in the sample, i.e. those for whom a complete questionnaire was filled in for all surveys.

In 1980, of the 4,882 couples included in the sample in 1966, data could be collected on 3,806 females. Of the 5,257 couples married in 1974 and included in the sample, questionnaires were filled in on 4,842 women in 1980. The data on ways of getting acquainted and on the housing conditions, fertility, family plans and the development of marriages at different durations of marriage are the results of the so-called cross-sectional processings carried out with the first method. However, the data on the relationship between housing conditions, on the one hand, and fertility and change in family plans, on the other hand, are the results of the second method, i.e. the so-called longitudinal method. These data refer to women who have continuously lived with their husband in their marriage contracted in 1966 and who have also participated in the follow-up surveys.

Bibliography

Balogh, M. 1979. "A nö helyzetének és szerepének alakulása a családban" [Development of the woman's situation and role in the family], in Demográfia (Budapest), No. 2-3, pp. 212-228.

David, H.P.; McIntyre, R.G. 1981. Reproductive behavior: Central and Eastern European experience. New York, Springer Publishing Co.

Demographic Research Institute. 1970-75. Family planning in Hungary: Main results of the 1966 Fertility and Family Planning (TCS) Study. Budapest.

Klinger, A. 1975a. "Az ujabb magyar családtervezési vizsgálatok föbb eredményei" [Main results of the recent Hungarian family planning studies, I], in Statisztikai Szemle (Budapest, Központi Statisztikai Hivatal), Feb. 1975.

--- .1975b. "Az ujabb magyar családtervezési vizsgálatok föbb eredményei" [Main results of the recent Hungarian family planning studies, II], in Statisztikai Szemle (Budapest, Központi Statisztikai Hivatal), Mar. 1975.

Központi Statisztikai Hivatal [Hungarian Central Statistical Office]. 1961. Demográfiai évkönyv, 1960 [Hungarian Demographic Yearbook, 1960]. Budapest.

--- .1963. A termékenységi, családtervezési és születésszabályozási vizsgálat fontosabb adatai [Main results of the Hungarian TCS study with English summary and headings]. Budapest.

--- .1965. "A nap 24 órája (12,000 ember napi időbeosztása)" [24 hours of the day: Daily distribution of time of 12,000 people], in Statisztikai Idöszaki Közlemények (Budapest), No. 75.

--- .1971. Demográfiai évkönyv, 1970 [Hungarian Demographic Yearbook, 1970]. Budapest.

--- .1976. Demográfiai évkönyv, 1975 [Hungarian Demographic Yearbook, 1975]. Budapest.

--- .1979a. Main results of the Hungarian fertility, family planning and birth control study, TCS-77, a preliminary report on the Hungarian study of the World Fertility Survey. Budapest, Statistical Publishing House.

--- .1979b. Az 1966-ban és 1974-ben házasságot kötöttek családtervezési termékenységi és születésszabályozási magatartása 1977-ig [Family planning, fertility and birth control attitudes of persons married in 1966 and 1974, until 1977]. Budapest, Statisztikai Kiadó Vállalat.

--- .1980a.   The Hungarian fertility survey, 1977: A summary of findings, World Fertility Survey No. 25 (Budapest), June 1980.

--- .1980b.   1980. évi népszámlálás: Részletes adatok a 2%-os képviseleti minta alapján [1980 Population Census: Detailed data on basis of a 2 per cent sample]. Budapest.

--- .1981a.   1970. évi népszámlálás: Termékenységi adatok [1970 Population Census: Fertility data]. Budapest.

--- .1981b. "Idömérleg" [Time budget, of the population aged 15-69 in 1976-77], in Társadalomstatisztikai Közlemények (Budapest).

--- .1981c.   1980. évi népszámlálás 21. Demográfiai adatok [1980 Population Census, 21, Demographic data]. Budapest.

--- .1981d. "A gyermekgondozási segély igénybevétele és hatásai (1967-80)" [Use and impact of the child-care allowance], in Statisztikai Idöszaki Közlemények, No. 492.

--- .1981e. "Életszinvonal, 1960-80" [Standard of living, 1960-80], in Statisztikai Idöszaki Közlemények (Budapest), No. 488.

--- .1982.   Demográfiai évkönyv, 1980 [Hungarian Demographic Year-book, 1980]. Budapest.

Molnár, E.; Pongrácz, M. 1980. "Népesedési kérdésekkel kapcsolatos közvéleménykutató vizsgálat" [Public opinion survey on population questions], in Központi Statisztikai Hivatal [Hungarian Central Statistical Office]: Népességtudományi Kutató Intézet Köleményei, No. 48.

Szalai, J. 1970. "A családi munkamegosztás néhány szociológiai kérdése" [Some sociological questions of the division of family work], in Valóság (Budapest), No. 10, pp. 43-55.

Vági, G. 1980.   Az otthoni munka és a társadalmilag szervezett tevékenységek viszonyának alakulása [Relation between home work and socially organised activities] (Budapest, A Központi Szolgáltatásfejlesztési Kutató Intézet kiadványa).